WOMEN'S CAR DIY

First published in September 2014

A catalogue record for this book is available from the British Library.

ISBN 978 0 85733 407 7

Published by Haynes Publishing,
Sparkford, Yeovil,
Somerset BA22 7JJ, UK.
Tel: 01963 442030 Fax: 01963 440001
Int. tel: +44 1963 442030
Int. fax: +44 1963 440001
E-mail: sales@haynes.co.uk
Website: www.haynes.co.uk

Haynes North America Inc.,
861 Lawrence Drive, Newbury Park,
California 91320, USA.

Printed in the USA by Odcombe Press LP,
1299 Bridgestone Parkway, La Vergne, TN 37086.

WOMEN'S CAR DIY

If you need something done, do it yourself

The Multi-Tasker's Manual

The girl's guide to car DIY including basic maintenance,
servicing and preparing for the MoT test

Caroline Lake

Contents

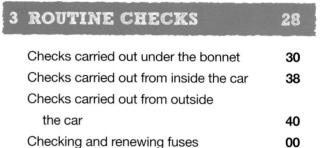

Introduction

Women have made significant progress in terms of equality over the last century, but when it comes to cars and garages, we seem stuck in the dark ages. Many women hate taking their car to a garage for fear of being intimidated, patronised or ripped off, and sadly this does occasionally still happen. I've been told by some women that they would rather go to the dentist than visit a garage!

Some unscrupulous garage staff love to 'blind' us with jargon, and see us as easy targets for extra cash. So you're told your 'diddlyflip' needs replacing at a cost of £500 – would you dare question the mechanic as to what it is or does, and why it needs replacing? Most women would just pay the bill regardless, and make a sharp exit. For this reason, where possible, many ladies will get a male

friend or relative to take their car to the garage for them.

Many women – and quite a few men – know nothing about their car, not even how to undo the bonnet, but I've discovered since working in the industry that there are lots of women who would like to learn more about their cars. They'd like to learn how to perform maintenance, what happens during a service, and so on, but they have no idea where to get the information. Well, actually it can be quite hard to find information, as there's very little in the way of publications aimed specifically at women – well, that is until now!

When Haynes Manuals approached me about writing a car DIY book for women, I was delighted. It was something I had been thinking about doing for a while, and seemed a natural progression from running a garage and teaching basic maintenance classes, so to be approached by the world's largest publisher of car books was a dream come true, and I leapt at the chance!

When I was a young child, my parents had old cars, 'bangers', that were always breaking down, and I hated it when they wouldn't start – it used to make me cry! I guess that was where my interest began, and as I got older I loved to help my Dad 'tinker'. By the time I was 14, while all my peers were reading the likes of *Smash Hits* magazine, I would have my head stuck in a car magazine or book, and I even memorised the 0–60mph times of every production car available in 1985 – how sad is that!

For my 16th birthday, my parents gave me a Triumph Dolomite as a minor restoration project. With the aid of a Haynes Manual and some help from my Dad, we got Dolly back on the road, and although she broke down at least once a month, I loved that car!

However, a career in the garage trade wasn't considered an option – I'm a girl! A stereotypical view which, sadly, is still present, but one which I am determined to change – women make fantastic mechanics!

My passion for cars stayed with me though, and some marketing work I did in my mid-twenties, for a garage that sold imported cars, was to further reinforce my desire to learn more about what makes cars tick. I soon set up a franchise with a Japanese company to import performance cars to order, to suit customers' exact requirements. I prided myself on offering a first-class service, and could explain the facts and figures. However, I wanted to know more about what I was selling, and be more hands-on before each car was passed to the customer. I could quote performance figures, but I would struggle to change a set of brake pads.

In a moment of bravery, I approached the garage that was carrying out preparation and servicing work for me at the time, and asked if I could go in one day a week as an unpaid apprentice and learn more about working on the cars. The owner thought it was a great laugh, but I duly bought boots and overalls, and so my career as a mechanic in the garage trade began.

Eventually, my perseverance and passion paid off, and I became a professional mechanic, which led to me taking my MoT tester's exam. Nobody, including my tutor, had ever heard of a woman tester before (I believe I was only the sixth in the country to qualify). This led to lots of women bringing their cars to me for that dreaded annual test, and I found that I loved showing them around their car, and explaining in simple terms what the parts were and, in some cases, why they had caused the car to fail an MoT. This planted an idea in my mind that there was a market for a female-friendly garage, which would allow me to help women gain confidence in the garage trade and teach them more about their cars.

The idea eventually became a business plan, and then reality in June 2006, when I opened the doors to Caroline's Cars. Since then, I've taught hundreds of women how to undo their car's bonnet, perform level checks, change a wheel, and much more. I also pride myself on offering an environment where women can have their cars maintained while feeling able to ask questions and knowing that they are going to be treated fairly.

Cars aren't rocket science ladies, although many people would have you believe otherwise! What happens during an MoT test or service isn't governed by the Official Secrets Act, and the thought of visiting a garage shouldn't fill you with dread and fear. There's no reason why you can't look after the basic maintenance of your car yourself, change a wheel, and much more if you want to. I hope that this book will give you the information and the confidence to do just that.

Whether you dip into the book from time to time to find the specific information you need, or read it from cover to cover to learn all about how your car works, I hope that, at the very least, I can provide you with sufficient knowledge and confidence that you will never feel intimidated or patronised when visiting a garage!

HOW A CAR WORKS

Although modern cars may at first seem very complicated, and are now fitted with many systems that are controlled by computer, few of the basic principles have changed since the car was invented in the 1800s. A car has an engine to power it, wheels that go round, steering to control its direction, and brakes to stop it! In addition, it has suspension to make the ride comfortable and to make the car more controllable, a transmission to take the power from the engine to the wheels, a fuel tank, and comfort items such as a ventilation/heater system to keep the occupants comfortable, and in-car entertainment.

Using simple terms and illustrations, this chapter explains where the various parts are located, and provides a jargon-free explanation of how they work. So ladies, what are you waiting for, turn the page and discover it's not as complicated as you thought after all!

The engine

When you lift the bonnet on a modern car, often you can't actually see much of the engine, as it tends to be hidden by plastic covers. What's underneath though, has changed very little since its invention. Known as the internal combustion engine, because the fuel is burnt inside the engine to produce the power, most engines run on petrol or diesel, although cars powered by Liquid Petroleum Gas (LPG) are increasingly common, and a few electric cars are beginning to appear on the roads.

Petrol and diesel engines are similar in lots of ways, the main difference between them being the way the fuel is ignited before it's burnt inside the engine. In a petrol engine there's a spark plug, which produces an electronic spark at just the right time to cause the fuel to ignite. In a diesel engine, the heat created by the air being compressed inside the engine sets light to the fuel.

All engines are divided into two main parts – a top part known as a cylinder head, and a bottom part known as a cylinder block. The cylinder head and block are separated by a special seal – known as a cylinder-head gasket (usually shortened to 'head gasket') – which provides a completely air- and fluid-tight seal between the two parts.

The cylinder block contains round chambers, open at both ends, known as cylinders, which have pistons inside them that move up and down. These pistons have metal rings around their tops (piston rings), which provide a gas- and fluid-tight seal to allow the pistons to move without letting gas or fluids leak past them.

The cylinder head houses the combustion chambers, which are where the air and fuel is burnt. Each cylinder has its own combustion chamber, and each combustion chamber has special 'doors' called

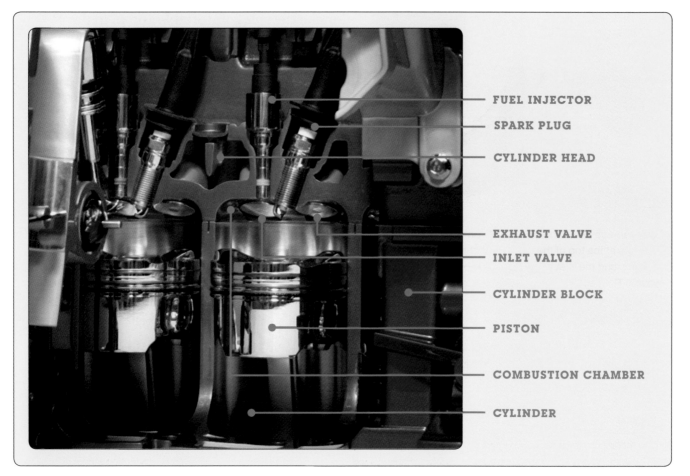

- FUEL INJECTOR
- SPARK PLUG
- CYLINDER HEAD
- EXHAUST VALVE
- INLET VALVE
- CYLINDER BLOCK
- PISTON
- COMBUSTION CHAMBER
- CYLINDER

valves, which open and close to allow air and fuel mixture into the cylinders (inlet valves), and exhaust gases out (exhaust valves), at just the right time to allow the engine to operate efficiently.

The bottom end of each piston is attached to a crankshaft, which turns the up-and-down motion of the pistons into the rotary motion needed to power the car's wheels.

You might have heard the term 'four-stroke'. This term comes from the fact that each piston moves up and down twice (up-down-up-down – hence four strokes), for each power-producing cycle of the engine. These four strokes are called 'induction', 'compression', 'power' and 'exhaust'. The four-stroke cycle is explained in more detail below.

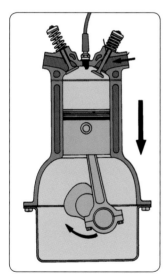

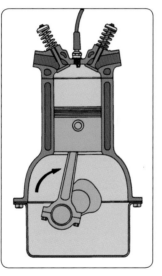

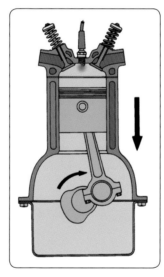

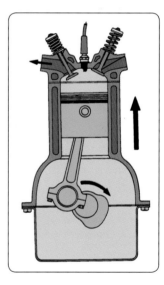

1. **Induction stroke** – The piston is at the top of the cylinder, and the inlet valve opens. The piston moves down to the bottom of the cylinder, sucking fuel and air in.

2. **Compression stroke** – When the piston reaches the bottom of the cylinder, the inlet valve closes and creates an air-tight chamber. The piston then rises to the top, squashing (compressing) the air and fuel into a small space in the combustion chamber.

3. **Power stroke** – The compressed fuel/air mixture is ignited, and the explosion forces the piston back down the cylinder. In a petrol engine, the mixture is ignited by a spark plug, and in a diesel, the mixture is ignited by the heat generated when the mixture is compressed.

4. **Exhaust stroke** – With the piston now back at the bottom of the cylinder, the cylinder is full of waste gases created by the burning of the mixture (exhaust gases). The exhaust valve opens, and the piston rises, pushing these gases out. Once the piston reaches the top of the cylinder, the exhaust valve closes, and the cycle begins again with another induction stroke.

The induction, compression, power and exhaust strokes are also sometimes known as 'suck, squeeze, bank, blow' – that must have been thought of by a bloke!

Engine management

Confused by the ECU or ECM, worried by the MIL light, and baffled by MAF and MAP sensors?

Although cars have become increasingly computer controlled, and now have very complex engine management systems, the basics of engine management – what it does and how it works – really aren't that complicated. However, engine management systems have become surrounded by jargon and confusion, sometimes fuelled by garages who would rather keep you in the dark and bewilder you with 'tech terms'.

The terms ECU (Electronic Control Unit) and ECM (Electronic Control Module) have exactly the same meaning, and are both terms for the 'brain' of your car's engine. This brain is fed information by various sensors on the car. It uses this information to adjust the air and fuel mixture and, in a petrol engine, the timing of the spark that ignites it. This fine control ensures that exhaust emissions are kept low, and also helps to provide the best fuel economy. Sensors also check that everything is working with the engine, and can pick up faults that may otherwise go undetected for some time.

The MIL (Malfunction Indicator Light), also known as the 'engine management' or 'check engine' light, tells the driver that a fault has been detected, and that the car needs to be plugged into specialist diagnostic equipment that will communicate with the ECU to find the problem. The ECU can store 'fault codes', which the technician can use to find out which sensor is indicating a fault. The most common problems are due to faults with the sensors themselves. Given the environment in which they work, over time they get dirty, hot, or simply worn out, and stop working correctly. Some examples of sensors, and what they do, are provided in the following section.

* Oxygen ('O2' or 'lambda') sensor – used to measure the amount of oxygen in the exhaust gases. This is important information for deciding the quantity of fuel the engine needs, and also for controlling exhaust emissions.
* TPS – Throttle Position Sensor, which measures the position and speed-of-change of position of the accelerator pedal.
* CTS – Coolant Temperature Sensor, which tells the ECU the engine temperature.
* CPS – Crankshaft Position Sensor, which calculates how fast the engine is turning, and can also provide information about the position of the engine's valves and pistons.

All the sensors are there to improve fuel economy, reduce emissions and provide optimum performance, and although finding and fixing a fault can sometimes be difficult, especially if it is an intermittent fault, a good technician should be able to solve any problems using the right diagnostic equipment.

Engine management sensors

You will often hear various sensors mentioned by technicians and mechanics, and the language used can be baffling. Here's a guide to some of the more common engine-management sensors, but be aware that different manufacturers often give them different names:

* MAF – Mass Air Flow sensor, which measures the amount of air going into the engine.
* MAP – Manifold Absolute Pressure sensor, which measures the pressure of the air going into the engine. This is used to calculate the density of the air, which is important information for deciding the quantity of fuel the engine needs.

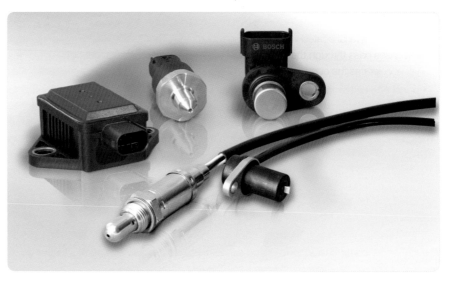

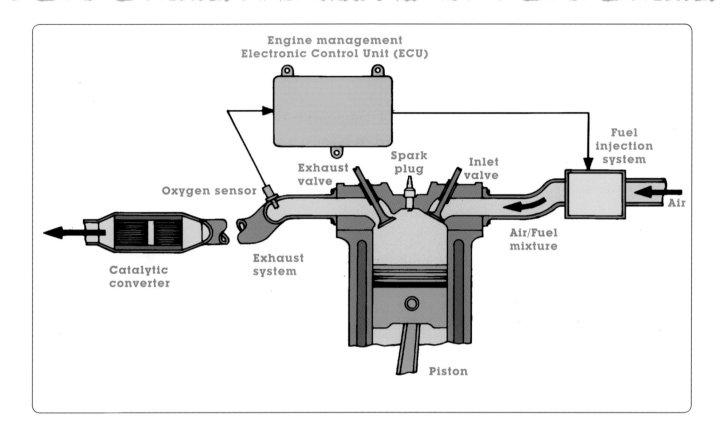

Engine management
Electronic Control Unit (ECU)

Oxygen sensor

Exhaust valve

Spark plug

Inlet valve

Fuel injection system

Air

Air/Fuel mixture

Catalytic converter

Exhaust system

Piston

Exhaust and emissions

The exhaust system provides a route for the exhaust gases to safely leave the engine. It may be made up of several different sections, depending on the car. It will also have at least one, often several, muffler (or 'silencer') boxes to reduce exhaust noise. An engine run without an exhaust can make a deafening noise! On petrol-engine cars, the exhaust will also contain a catalytic converter, and on many diesel engine cars, a Diesel Particulate Filter (DPF).

A catalytic converter consists of a steel canister containing a honeycomb material coated with various special metals. The exhaust gases pass through the catalytic converter, where the catalyst accelerates the conversion of harmful gases into harmless gases and water vapour.

An oxygen sensor is fitted to the exhaust. On most newer cars there are two oxygen sensors, one before the catalytic converter and one after. These detect the amount of oxygen in the exhaust gases and feed the information back to the engine management system, which adjusts the air/fuel mixture entering the engine to control emissions, and improve fuel economy.

A Diesel Particulate Filter (DPF) is fitted to the exhaust of all current diesel cars to remove soot particles from the exhaust gases. These filters have been a legal requirement since 2009, but many vehicles were fitted with them before this. Over time, a DPF clogs up with ash, and can cause engine-running problems. The filter is often designed to clean itself in a process known as regeneration. Some cars have a reservoir next to the fuel tank containing a DPF additive. Tiny amounts of this fluid are automatically added to the fuel when you fill up to aid regeneration. You can also buy DPF cleaning additive to put in the fuel tank. As high temperatures are required to cause regeneration, cars that do lots of short journeys often end up with clogged filters, as they don't get hot. To try and 'encourage' a blocked filter to regenerate itself, take the car for a run of at least 10 miles (16km) to get it up to a high temperature.

CATALYTIC CONVERTER

Transmission

Transmission is the term used for the group of components that transmit power from the engine to the car's wheels. Often, just the gearbox is considered to be the transmission, but the term actually applies to all the components involved between the engine and the wheels. The components used depend on whether the car has the front wheels, rear wheels, or all four wheels driven. As well as the manual or automatic gearbox itself, they include a clutch (manual transmission only), driveshafts, and, on rear-wheel-drive and four-wheel-drive cars, a propeller shaft (or shafts), which runs under the middle of the car and transmits drive to the rear wheels (and sometimes the front wheels too on a four-wheel-drive car).

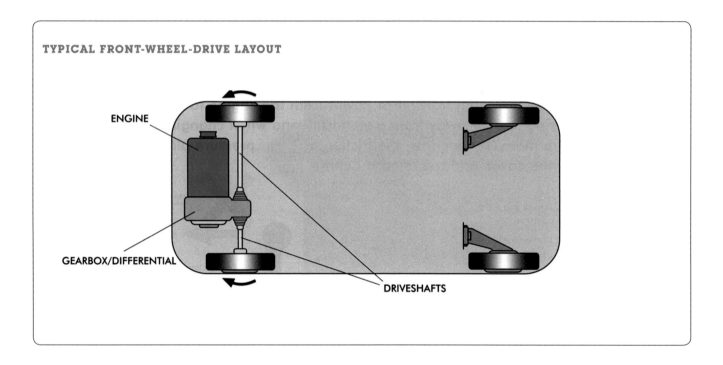

TYPICAL FRONT-WHEEL-DRIVE LAYOUT

ENGINE

GEARBOX/DIFFERENTIAL

DRIVESHAFTS

Clutch

The clutch (manual-gearbox cars) allows power to be transferred smoothly from the engine to the transmission when moving away from a standstill, and when changing gear. It also allows you to disconnect the engine from the transmission so you can have the engine running without the car moving (neutral). The clutch engages and disengages from something known as a flywheel, bolted to the end of the engine crankshaft, and transfers the power to the gearbox.

Manual gearbox

A manual gearbox allows the driver to select the best gear to suit the car's speed and the road conditions. A bit like a bicycle, the different-sized gears allow you to travel at different speeds and deal with the extra effort required to climb hills etc.

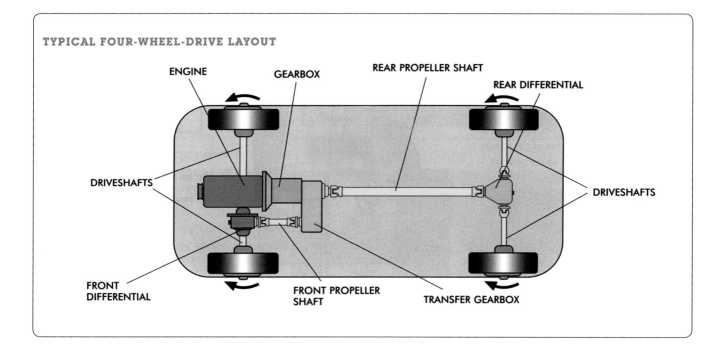

TYPICAL FOUR-WHEEL-DRIVE LAYOUT

ENGINE

GEARBOX

REAR PROPELLER SHAFT

REAR DIFFERENTIAL

DRIVESHAFTS

DRIVESHAFTS

FRONT DIFFERENTIAL

FRONT PROPELLER SHAFT

TRANSFER GEARBOX

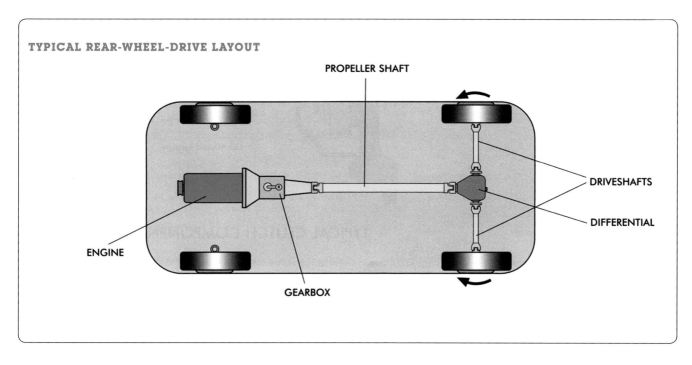

TYPICAL REAR-WHEEL-DRIVE LAYOUT

PROPELLER SHAFT

DRIVESHAFTS

DIFFERENTIAL

ENGINE

GEARBOX

Automatic transmission

There are two different types of automatic transmission, a conventional automatic transmission and Continuously Variable Transmission (CVT). Both types operate using a hydraulic control system that receives signals from various sensors on the car, eliminating the need for the driver to change gear. Automatic transmissions are much more complicated than manual ones, and usually have an electronic control unit (brain), to control them.

Driveshafts

A driveshaft transmits the power to the driven wheels. A large majority of modern cars are front-wheel drive, meaning that only the front wheels are driven by the engine. In this case, there are two driveshafts, one on each side, running from the gearbox (or automatic transmission) to each of the front wheels. Rear-wheel-drive cars have a driveshaft running to each of the rear wheels, and on a four-wheel-drive car there are four driveshafts, one for each wheel.

Suspension and steering

The suspension has two jobs – to keep the tyres in contact with the road, enabling the driver to control the car; and to cushion the car's occupants from bumps in the road, providing a comfortable ride. The steering is carefully designed to work in conjunction with the suspension.

The design of the suspension is always a compromise, because the characteristics needed to give a comfortable ride generally won't give good handling, and vice versa. For a comfortable ride, a reasonably soft suspension is needed to cushion the car's body from bumps in the road surface. For good handling, a stiff suspension is needed to keep all four tyres in contact with the road, and to keep the car's body as stable as possible.

The suspension on most cars uses a combination of springs and shock absorbers (or 'dampers') to help absorb road shocks and to control the up-and-down movement of the wheels. The suspension components are mounted on the body using insulating rubbers to reduce the transmission of shocks, noise and vibration from the suspension to the body.

Suspension systems are very precisely designed, and springs and shock absorbers are carefully chosen to suit the weight and handling characteristics of the particular model of car. Worn or damaged suspension components will affect the handling and braking of the car, and can be very dangerous. Worn components can also cause noises, such as clonks and rattles, when driving, especially when going over a bump.

© BMW Press

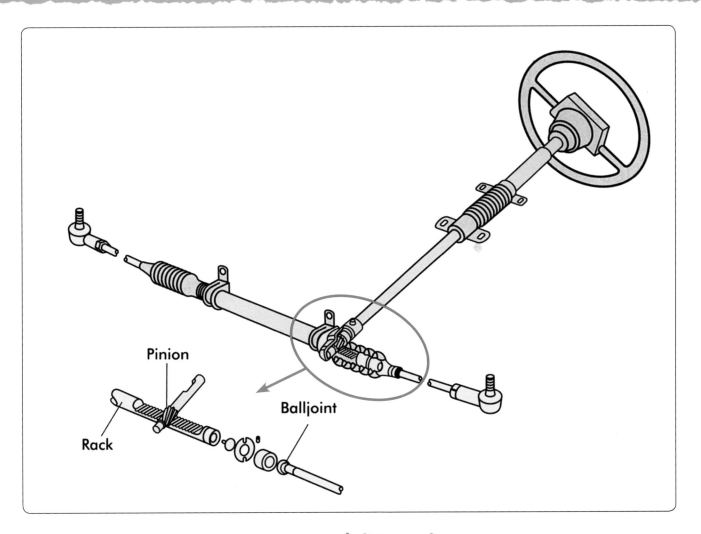

Pinion

Balljoint

Rack

Worn shock absorbers

When shock absorbers wear, it will result in poor handling and braking, because the car's body will move more than usual, and the wheels will tend to bounce when they hit bumps. Worn shock absorbers on your car can also increase your stopping distance by up to 20 per cent. For these reasons, driving a car with worn shock absorbers can be very dangerous.

To check your car's shock absorbers, press down and then release each corner of the car in turn. The corner of the car should move back up to its original position, and then settle. If the suspension rises up and bounces when you let go, or if you hear a hissing or knocking sound as the suspension moves, the shock absorber is probably worn or faulty, and you should have your car checked at your local garage or a specialist centre as soon as possible.

Steering

Steering systems have to be carefully designed to work in conjunction with the suspension. The steering system must allow the driver to keep the car pointing straight ahead, even when driving over bumps, and the driver must be able to steer the car without too much effort.

The main components of the steering system are the steering wheel, the steering column, the steering gear and the track rods. The steering column connects the steering wheel to the steering gear. The steering gear (often called a 'steering rack') transforms the rotary movement of the steering wheel into a linear (side-to-side) movement to move the car's wheels, and the track rods connect the steering gear to the wheels.

Many cars are fitted with power steering, to make it easier for the driver to turn the steering wheel. Some heavy cars with wide, low-profile tyres would be almost impossible to steer at low speeds without power steering. Some power-steering systems use hydraulic pressure to increase the effort applied to the steering wheel by the driver, with an engine-driven pump supplying the hydraulic pressure. Increasingly, newer cars use an electric power-steering system.

Brakes

The brakes work using hydraulic pressure to force friction material against a rotating metal disc or drum connected to each wheel. Friction slows the disc or drum – the harder you press the pedal, the more quickly the car slows down.

Anti-lock Braking System (ABS)

If you press really hard, for example in an emergency situation, there is a chance that the brakes could stop the wheels from rotating altogether, causing the car to skid. Because of this, most cars are now fitted with an Anti-lock Braking System (ABS). Sensors are fitted to each wheel, which detect when the brakes are about to lock. The ABS unit then releases and re-applies the brakes many times per second to allow the wheel to continue rotating and make sure the driver keeps control.

PADS

CALIPER

DISC

Brake hydraulic systems

The brakes on all modern cars are operated by a hydraulic system, which increases the pressure the driver applies to the brake pedal, to operate the brake at each wheel. The system contains a component known as a 'servo', which multiplies the effort that the driver applies to the brake pedal.

The brake pedal operates a piston inside a master cylinder full of fluid. When the pedal is pressed, the piston moves, pushing the fluid from the master cylinder along a narrow brake pipe. The fluid moves a second piston at the other end of the pipe, which operates the brake. The master cylinder has four pipes connected to it – one for the brake on each wheel – so that the brakes on all four wheels are operated simultaneously.

If there's a leak in the hydraulic system, fluid can escape, so the brakes won't work properly. As a safety measure, the hydraulic system is split into two separate circuits, with two pedal-operated pistons in a single master cylinder. Usually, each circuit operates one front brake and the rear brake diagonally opposite, so that if one of the circuits develops a leak, the car will still stop in a straight line. However, this split-circuit safety system will only work until all the brake fluid has escaped, which won't take long!

Braking systems must be maintained properly to ensure safety. The fluid in the braking system deteriorates with age, and it must be renewed at the manufacturer's recommended intervals – usually every two years.

Handbrake (or 'parking brake')

The handbrake is usually operated by a hand-operated lever, but on some cars, such as certain Mercedes, it's operated by a foot pedal or, increasingly, by an electronic button or switch. Usually, the handbrake works by applying the rear brakes mechanically via a cable, although electrically operated handbrakes often don't have a cable. Either way, the handbrake operates independently of the brake hydraulic system.

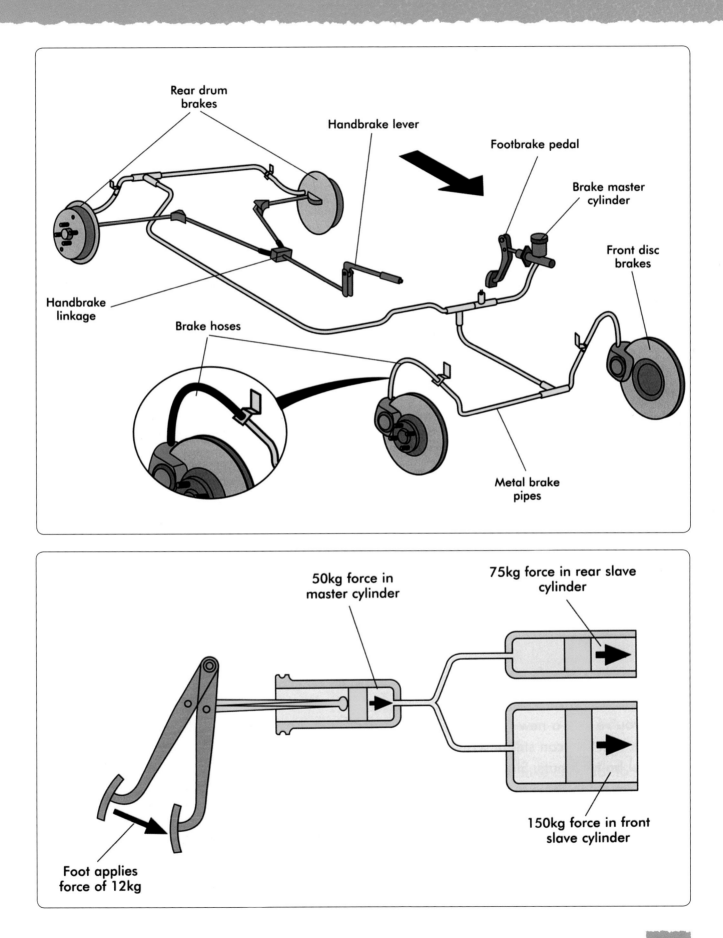

Rear drum
brakes

Handbrake lever

Footbrake pedal

Brake master
cylinder

Front disc
brakes

Handbrake
linkage

Brake hoses

Metal brake
pipes

50kg force in
master cylinder

75kg force in rear slave
cylinder

150kg force in front
slave cylinder

Foot applies
force of 12kg

Electrical systems

The electrical system on all modern cars consists of a 12-volt battery, an alternator, a starter motor, and various electrical accessories, components and wiring. There is also one or more Electronic Control Unit (ECU), and various sensors that send information to the ECU(s). ECUs control systems such as the engine management system, automatic transmission, the central-locking system, and the car's safety system (air bags and seatbelt tensioners).

Wiring looms

To simplify a car's wiring, and to make it more reliable, the wiring is normally arranged in 'looms'. The wiring looms are connected together using large multi-plug connectors, and the wires inside each loom are wrapped with cloth tape or plastic sheathing to protect them against chafing and accidental damage. To cut down on costs, often only one or two different types of wiring loom are made for a particular car model range, regardless of the standard equipment and options fitted. This means that sometimes there will be wiring connectors hanging from the loom that aren't used – for example, there may be wiring connectors for front fog lights, but front fog lights may not be fitted to all models – so don't worry if you find a mysterious connector dangling somewhere, which doesn't seem to be connected to anything!

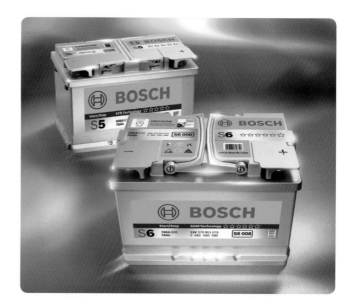

The battery

The battery acts as an electrical reservoir, supplying electricity to operate the car's electrical systems. When the engine is running, the battery is charged constantly by the alternator (see following section), but when the engine is stopped – for example when starting the car – the battery has to supply all the electrical power. Most modern cars have a lot of electrical equipment fitted, which means that there's a heavy load on the battery. The original batteries fitted to cars are almost always 'maintenance-free'. Most batteries are supplied with a guarantee, and as a rough guide a battery should normally last at least three or four years under normal conditions before it needs to be replaced.

The alternator

Once the engine's running, the alternator – which is driven from the engine by a belt – supplies the electricity to operate the various electrical systems (engine-management system, lights, electric windows, instruments, etc), and keeps the battery fully charged. A faulty alternator may not charge the battery properly, and may cause a flat battery. If the alternator is faulty, the 'charge warning' light on the dashboard will usually come on – in this case get the car checked as soon as possible.

ALTERNATOR

The starter motor

The starter motor is a very powerful electric motor, which engages with a toothed 'flywheel' attached to the engine crankshaft to spin the engine until it starts. When the ignition key is turned, a solenoid (electrically operated lever) in the starter pushes out a gear to engage with the flywheel. The starter then spins the flywheel. Once the engine starts, the solenoid switches off and the starter motor disengages.

Fuses and relays

Fuses and relays are vital components of the electrical system. Fuses are used to protect electrical components and circuits against damage from high loads when there's a fault in the circuit. They consist of a wire of an exact thickness that's designed to melt and break the circuit when the electrical current exceeds a set level – which is what usually happens if there's a short circuit in a wire or component. The main fuses are usually located in a fuse box inside the car, and can be easily replaced (see Chapter 3).

Relays are used as switches in electrical circuits. If a component needs a high current to operate it, it will need thick wiring to cope with the current. To avoid having to use a lot of thick wiring throughout the car, relays are used. A relay is a solenoid that operates one or more sets of electrical contacts. The high current is passed to the contacts, and a low current is used to operate the solenoid. This means that thinner wiring can be used in the circuit from the switch to the relay.

STARTER MOTOR

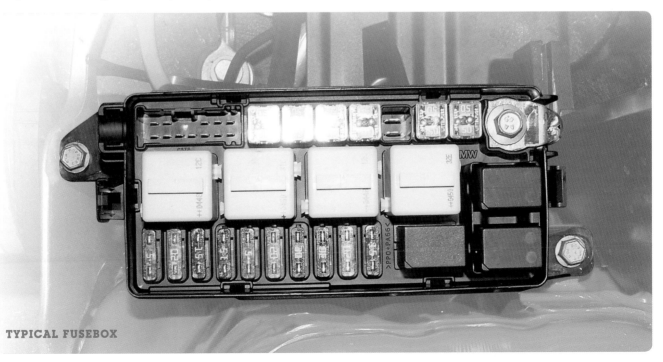

TYPICAL FUSEBOX

TOOLS AND EQUIPMENT

This chapter explains about some of the tools you may need when working on your car, and also some of the tools and other items that it's worth carrying in the car in case of emergencies. We all hope that we'll never break down, be in an accident, or get stranded by the weather, but having an emergency kit in the boot, just in case you have a problem, can make the situation easier to deal with.

Emergency kit to keep in your boot

It's a good idea to have an emergency kit, including a few tools, in the boot in case of an accident or breakdown. Even if you encounter a problem you can't fix yourself, someone else might be able to help you if you can supply a spanner! In fact, it's worth noting that in some countries it's compulsory to carry certain items, such as a warning triangle, first aid kit, high-visibility jacket, spare bulbs and fuses, and possibly even a breathalyser kit!

Here's a selection of items which you might want to carry – the list could go on forever, but it's a case of striking a balance between taking up too much space in your boot, and having the necessary items to get you out of trouble. A tool bag or holdall will help to keep everything together and safe. Car accessory shops sell bags designed for this purpose. Many tools and accessories are available in pink, which adds some extra fun!

* **Warning triangle** – this will help to warn other motorists if you break down, and is compulsory when driving in some countries abroad.

* **Wheel brace with extending handle** – this can be invaluable if you have a puncture and need to change a wheel. The brace supplied with the car is usually very short, and even the strongest of men have been unable to change a wheel using one! Make sure you buy a good quality one – cheap ones can break!

* **First aid kit** – compact kits designed especially to keep in your car can be bought cheaply from many outlets.

* **Spare bulbs and fuses** – you can buy the appropriate kit for your car in most car accessory shops.

* **Fire extinguisher** – a compact extinguisher designed especially for vehicles can be bought from car accessory shops.

* **Selection of cable ties** – these have a multitude of uses.

* **Roll of insulating tape** – this can come in useful for emergency wiring repairs and many other jobs.

* **Roll of gaffer tape (sometimes called 'duct' tape)** – this is an amazing product. You can hold almost anything together with it. Make sure you buy good-quality tape – the cheap imitations don't stick!

* **Selection of hose clips** – for emergency hose repairs.

* **Can of water-dispersant spray (such as WD-40)** – can help to solve problems with damp electrical components, and can help move rusty fixings.

* **Luggage restraints (elastic 'bungee' type)** – self-explanatory!

* **High-visibility vest** – will keep you safe if you break down, and compulsory in some countries abroad.

* **Tyre pressure gauge** – for carrying out your weekly tyre check.

* **Tyre tread-depth gauge** – as above.

* **Foot pump or tyre inflator** – you can buy a mini compressor which you plug into your cigarette lighter socket. These are affordable, compact, and are easy to operate.

* **Pliers** – an invaluable multipurpose tool.

* **Compact tool kit** – you can buy a compact basic tool kit, which contains items such as screwdrivers, spanners and sockets, to keep in your car.

* **Torch** – the wind-up variety is a great idea for the boot, as you never have to worry about the batteries going flat!

* **A clean cloth** – invaluable!

* **Disposable gloves** – essential.

* **Travel pack of baby wipes** – to clean your hands, even if you haven't been working on your car!

IN WINTER, IT'S ALSO A GOOD IDEA TO CARRY THE FOLLOWING:
* Windscreen de-icer spray.
* Ice scraper.
* Blanket.
* Woolly hat and gloves.
* Folding snow shovel.
* A bottle of water and some chocolate or other snack, in case you get stranded for a long time.

DIY Tools

The tool kit supplied with most cars won't allow you to do much more than change a wheel, and sometimes it's not even sufficient for that! Depending on how much maintenance you plan to do, you may only need a few items – if you only want to perform the routine checks, then the tools suggested for the emergency kit in the previous section will be sufficient. If you decide to get more adventurous and perform servicing and more complicated maintenance, then you'll need a more comprehensive set of tools.

You don't need to buy the most expensive tools, but generally you get what you pay for, and a good-quality set of tools will last for many years. Most car accessory shops and many online shops stock mechanic's tools kits, which contain most, if not all, of the tools you might need.

If in doubt about which tool to use, or how to tackle a particular job, don't attempt it without taking advice from an experienced friend, or consulting the Haynes Manual for your car, which will contain all the information you need.

Safety first!

Before you begin maintaining your car, it's important to consider health and safety. Make sure that you wear suitable protective clothing, known nowadays as PPE (Personal Protective Equipment). PPE should be considered the most important part of your tool kit. Also take care to avoid catching long hair or jewellery in rotating parts if the engine is running.

The following items are essential:

* Overalls, or similar protective clothing.
* Disposable gloves.
* Goggles, or safety glasses.
* Steel-toe-capped boots are also a sensible precaution, and are available in a number of designs and colours – including pink of course!

You also need to carefully consider fire risks, and a fire extinguisher is essential.

Ensure that the car won't fall on you or roll away. If you have to raise the car, always use wheel chocks and axle stands, and never ever work under a car supported only by a jack, as it could fail and cause the car to fall on you.

Think about tripping and slipping hazards – always clean up any spills as soon as they happen, and clear tools away.

It's not a good idea to carry out anything other than the simplest maintenance jobs when you're alone. Get a friend to come along and supply the tea, or help out and join in the fun!

Servicing tool kit

For general maintenance work on your car, you'll probably need these items in addition to those already suggested for your in-car emergency tool kit.

* **Socket set, spanner set and screwdriver set** – you'll be able to carry out most of the work you're likely to need to do on your car with these three items. As mentioned previously, you can buy a compact tool kit that will contain a selection of these tools in a range of sizes.
* **Torx bits and Allen keys** – these tools are needed to undo fixings on many modern cars. Again, they are included in many tool kits.
* **Adjustable spanner** – these have a multitude of uses, and can be helpful around the house too.
* **Pliers** – long-nose and normal versions will cover most jobs.
* **Hammer** – it's a good idea to have copper-faced, rubber-faced and metal ones for different uses. Using a metal hammer in certain situations – such as removing a seized wheel – can cause damage.
* **Small wire brush** – for removing corrosion and cleaning battery terminals.
* **Abrasive paper** – as above.
* **Spray grease** – for lubricating locks and hinges.
* **Torque wrench** – for correctly tightening important fixings. The Haynes Manual for your car will specify the correct torque-wrench settings.
* **Torch** – to light the way!

If you're planning to carry out basic servicing, you'll also need the following:

* Hydraulic jack.
* Axle stands, or car ramps.
* Oil filter removal tool – there are many different types, so check which one is best for your car.
* Oil sump drain plug tool – a socket is all that's needed on some cars, but others may require a specialist tool.
* Funnel – for pouring fluids.
* Oil draining container – DIY oil drainers are available cheaply, and make renewing the oil easier and less messy.
* Spark plug socket (only needed for petrol-engined cars) – make sure you buy the correct size for the spark plugs on your car.
* Small mirror – very handy for looking at hard-to-see items, and for finding things you've dropped!
* Mechanic's crawler – this is a board on wheels to allow you to roll in and out from under the car.
* Kneeling/lying down mat – makes kneeling and lying so much more comfortable!
* Antifreeze tester – checks the level of antifreeze protection in the coolant.
* Brake-fluid tester – checks the water content of the brake fluid, so you know when the fluid needs to be renewed.
* The Haynes Manual for your particular car is a great addition to your tool kit, and will guide you safely and easily through the various procedures.

If you decide to carry out more advanced maintenance or repair jobs, you'll need some additional tools, and you can add to your tool kit as you progress. Where an expensive, specialist tool is required for a certain job, it may be more cost effective to pay someone to carry out the work for you.

www.carparts-direct.co.uk

ROUTINE CHECKS

Carrying out your own routine checks and maintenance is much simpler than you might imagine. Regular checks can save you money, help you to spot potential problems, and will ensure that your car is safe and legal. The checks and tasks covered in this chapter are all simple to carry out, and should ideally be carried out once a week, or before you start a long journey. You won't need any special tools for these jobs.

Weekly checks list

* Engine oil.
* Coolant.
* Brake fluid.
* Power steering fluid.
* Windscreen washer fluid.
* Wiper blades.
* Washer jets.
* Battery.
* Tyres.
* Lights.

Checks carried out under the bonnet

Most of the checks in the list on the previous page can be carried out under the bonnet of your car. They are very simple, should take no more than 10 minutes, and will help keep your car in tip-top condition!

First, we need to open the bonnet. If you've never opened it before, then locating the bonnet-release lever for your car could be the most difficult job on this page! See the *'Opening the bonnet'* panel for details of how to open the bonnet.

With the bonnet open and safely supported, you can now carry out the under-bonnet checks. It's a good idea to wear disposable gloves for these checks.

Opening the bonnet

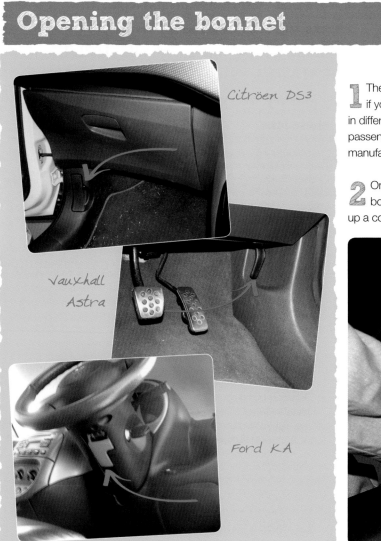

Citroën DS3

Vauxhall Astra

Ford KA

1 The location of the lever will be given in your car's handbook, if you have it. Different manufacturers put the release lever in different places, but it's normally either in the driver's or passenger's footwell, or sometimes under the steering wheel. Some manufacturers do a particularly good job of hiding them!

2 Once you've located the lever, give it a sharp pull to release the bonnet – you should hear a click and the bonnet should pop up a couple of centimetres.

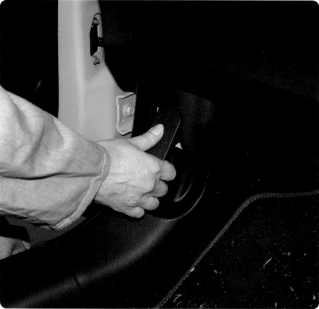

3 For safety reasons there's also a secondary bonnet catch fitted, which again can be quite fiddly to find. It may be under the bonnet, in which case you will need to slip your fingers inside the gap between the bonnet and the car's front panel to find a lever, which you may have to lift, or push to the side, with one hand as you lift the bonnet with the other. Alternatively, a lever may pop out of the front grille panel, which you may need to pull to release the catch.

4 Once you have the bonnet open, you may find that it will open fully by itself and is supported on gas struts, like the boot or tailgate, or you may need to use a bonnet stay (or 'prop') to hold it open. The bonnet stay is a metal rod, hinged to the bonnet or the car body at one end, and usually clipped in place at the other end to stop it rattling.

5 You'll need to unclip the free end of the bonnet stay and look for a specially designed locating hole or bracket on the bonnet or body, as applicable, to clip it into.

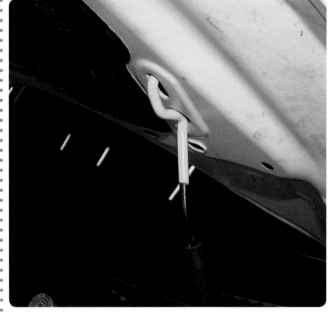

6 Sometimes, this hole or bracket is not immediately obvious, but if you lift the bonnet fully open, you should be able to work out where the bonnet stay fits.

Bonnet release on some Ford cars

On some Ford cars, you'll need to move the badge on the front grille panel and use the ignition key to operate the bonnet release! Turn the badge to reveal a slot for the key, then turn the key one way to release the first catch, and the opposite way to release the secondary catch.

Checking the engine oil

Checking the oil level is one of the most important checks you'll ever carry out on your car. Having the right quantity of oil in your engine is vital, as oil lubricates the moving parts, and if the level becomes too low, expensive engine damage can be caused. In the worst case, the engine may stop, in which case terminal engine damage has probably been caused!

The oil level is checked using a dipstick, which fits down inside a reservoir at the bottom of the engine, called the sump, into which the oil drains when the engine has stopped.

To check the oil level, proceed as follows:

TO CHECK THE ENGINE OIL, YOU'LL NEED:

* A clean cloth.
* A funnel.
* A pack of engine oil of the correct type and grade for your engine.

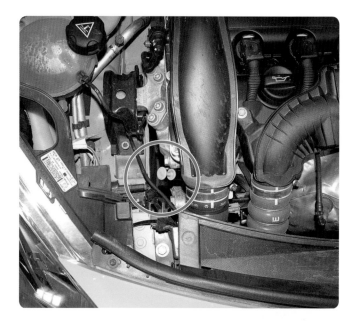

1 Park the car on level ground, make sure the engine has been stopped for at least five minutes, then open the bonnet and find the oil level dipstick. The location of the dipstick will vary depending on the model of car, but your car handbook or Haynes Manual will tell you where it is if you're unsure. The top of the dipstick is often brightly coloured to help you to find it.

2 Pull the dipstick completely out of its tube, then wipe the oil off using a clean cloth, push the dipstick slowly all the way back into the tube, then pull it out again and check the oil level. The bottom of the dipstick will have level markings, usually in the form of lines or notches towards its bottom. The oil level should be between the upper and lower marks. If the level is near the lower mark, you need to top up.

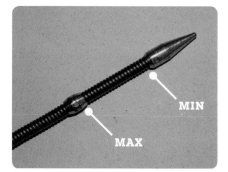

MIN

MAX

3 To top up, find the oil filler cap – check your car's handbook or Haynes Manual for its location. The cap is normally (but not always) clearly marked, and is usually on the top of the engine. It's very important to use the correct type of oil for your particular car – again, your owner's handbook or Haynes Manual should tell you which oil to use, and on some cars the correct oil type is marked under the bonnet (also see the panel 'Choosing engine oil'). If you're in any doubt, contact your vehicle manufacturer, and they will tell you.

4 Remove the oil filler cap – some caps unscrew and others are a push-fit – and pour in a little oil, 100ml or so to start with. A funnel will help to avoid spills.

Engine oil

It's vital to use the correct grade of oil in your car's engine, as serious damage can be caused by using the wrong grade.

There are three basic types of engine oil. The cheaper oils are usually 'mineral-based' and are suitable for providing basic protection for older cars. The mid-price oils are usually 'semi-synthetic' and are good 'in-between' oils, and the expensive oils are 'fully synthetic', providing the ultimate in engine protection.

The two main things to look for in the oil specification are the 'viscosity' (thickness) grade, which is shown by the 'SAE' rating, and the oil quality, indicated by the 'API' or 'ACEA' rating. These specifications will be marked on the oil packaging, and most well-known brands will be suitable. If the packaging doesn't have any specifications marked on it, don't buy it!

5 Wait a few seconds for the oil to drain down to the bottom of the engine, then re-check the oil level on the dipstick (repeat step 2). If the level is still below the upper mark, repeat the topping-up procedure until the level reaches the mark. Don't overfill the engine with oil, as this can cause leaks and possibly damage.

6 When you've finished, refit the filler cap tightly, wipe away any spills, and make sure that the dipstick is pushed all the way into its tube.

If you get into the habit of checking the oil level regularly, you will soon learn how much oil your car uses. If all's well with your car's engine, you should rarely have to top up the oil. If you need to top up on a regular basis, get your car checked by your local garage.

Checking the engine coolant

The coolant is vital, because it stops your car's engine from overheating. It also provides a source of heat for the in-car heater. Coolant is a mixture of water and antifreeze, which is circulated around the engine by a pump.

To check the coolant level you'll need to locate the coolant reservoir under the bonnet. This is usually a white, semi-transparent plastic bottle, but different manufacturers use different designs and locations, so if you're unsure, consult your owner's handbook or Haynes Manual. It's important to check the level when the engine is cool, as heat causes the coolant to expand, so if you have driven your car recently, you'll need to let the engine cool down before you can check the coolant level accurately. Coolant normally has a coloured dye added, so it should be easy to identify.

To check the coolant level, proceed as follows:

1 Firstly, make sure that the car is parked on level ground, then find the coolant reservoir. Check your car's handbook or Haynes Manual if you're not sure where it is.

Antifreeze

Antifreeze should be used in the cooling system all year round, even in the summer. This is because antifreeze doesn't just prevent the coolant from freezing in winter (which could cause serious engine damage); it also prevents water from corroding the metal parts of the engine. Antifreeze is poisonous, therefore care should be taken when handling it, and gloves are a must.

If the coolant is a nasty brown, rusty colour, it will need to be renewed, as it's unlikely to provide sufficient protection for the engine. Coolant renewal is a procedure easily carried out by your local garage – they will drain the system, clean it by flushing the system, and then refill with fresh water and antifreeze.

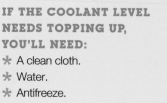

IF THE COOLANT LEVEL NEEDS TOPPING UP, YOU'LL NEED:
* A clean cloth.
* Water.
* Antifreeze.

2 The reservoir will normally have maximum and minimum level marks on the side – ensure the coolant level is between the marks.

3 The cooling system works under high pressure, so if you do need to top up, make sure the engine is cool. NEVER remove the filler cap if the engine is hot. Place a rag over the filler cap to protect your hands, and slowly unscrew the cap, as there may still be pressure in the system, even if the engine is cool.

4 Using a jug or bottle, top up the level to the maximum mark using a 50/50 mixture of clean water and antifreeze. If you need to top up a large amount, or you need to top up often, this may indicate a problem, such as a split hose or a leaky radiator, so get a garage to check to see if there's a problem.

5 When you've finished topping up, refit the filler cap tightly.

Checking the brake fluid

The brake fluid reservoir is usually a white plastic bottle, which will have minimum (or 'Min') and maximum (or 'Max') levels marked on it. Because the bottle is semi-transparent and the fluid is a light golden colour, it should be easy to see the level.

It's very important for safety to check the brake fluid level regularly. As your car's brakes wear, the fluid level will slowly go down over a period of months or years, and as long as the fluid level is at least halfway between 'Min' and 'Max' marks, this is fine. However, if you notice a sudden drop, or if the level falls below the 'Min' mark, top the level up to the 'Max' mark and take your car to a mechanic as soon as possible, as there's likely to be a fault – probably a fluid leak, which in the worst case could result in brake failure.

The brake fluid reservoir also contains a sensor to detect low fluid level. If the low-brake-fluid-level warning light on the dashboard comes on, stop as soon as possible, check the level and top up.

To check the brake fluid level, proceed as follows:

1 Make sure that the car is parked on level ground, then find the brake fluid reservoir. Check your car's handbook or Haynes Manual if you're not sure where it is.

2 Make sure that the fluid level is close to the 'Max' mark.

3 If you need to top up, slowly unscrew the cap from the reservoir. Some fluid reservoirs have a small float attached to the cap, which operates the low-fluid-level warning light. If the cap has a float, remove the cap very slowly so that the fluid can drain from the float back into the reservoir before you lift it out. Sometimes, you may have to disconnect the fluid-level sensor wiring plug from the cap to allow the cap to be removed. Place the cap and float on a clean cloth to catch any drips.

4 Top up with clean, new brake fluid to bring the level up to the 'Max' mark. If the cap has a float attached to it, bear in mind that the float will cause the fluid level to rise when you refit the cap, so allow for this when topping up.

5 Screw the cap back on to the reservoir, ensuring you wipe away any spills straight away. If you get brake fluid on your skin, wash it off immediately.

Brake fluid

If you need to top up the brake fluid, it's not necessarily due to a leak. As the brake pads wear, the fluid level will naturally drop, which is no cause for concern. This drop in fluid level will take place over a long period of time. If you need to top up the fluid level every week, this is probably due to a leak, and you should have the braking system checked by a mechanic as soon as possible.

Brake fluid is a special hydraulic fluid designed specifically for use in car braking systems. Most cars use a specification of fluid known as 'DOT 4'. Brake fluid is hygroscopic, which means it absorbs moisture over time. Moisture in the braking system can affect its efficiency, and will cause deterioration of the brake fluid, and that's why most manufacturers recommend changing the brake fluid every two years. Because it absorbs moisture, brake fluid should always be stored in a closed, air-tight container.

Checking the power steering fluid

IF THE POWER STEERING FLUID LEVEL NEEDS TOPPING UP, YOU'LL NEED:

* A clean cloth.
* Power steering fluid of the correct type.

Hydraulic clutches

Some cars have a hydraulically operated clutch, which may have a separate fluid reservoir, although some hydraulic clutches have a sealed fluid system, with no reservoir.

Check your car's handbook or Haynes Manual to see if your car is fitted with a hydraulic clutch, and whether the fluid level needs checking. If it does, the procedure will be similar to the brake fluid level checking procedure.

A leak in the clutch hydraulic circuit can cause the clutch to fail.

Many cars nowadays have power steering, and this is often electrically operated, in which case there will be no fluid to check. However, if your car has hydraulic power steering, you will need to check the fluid level regularly. Different manufacturers use different systems and locations for the reservoir, so check with your car's handbook or Haynes Manual for the reservoir location.

Some power steering fluid reservoirs are dark coloured, and have a level dipstick attached to the inside of the filler cap, while others have a transparent reservoir with markings on the outside, similar to a brake fluid reservoir. Sometimes there are 'HOT' and 'COLD' level markings for use depending on whether the engine is hot or cold.

To check the power steering fluid level, proceed as follows:

1 Check that the car is parked on level ground, and look for the power steering reservoir. Check your car's handbook or Haynes Manual for the location.

2 If you need to remove the reservoir cap to check the level, wipe around the cap, then unscrew it, and check that the level is up to the appropriate mark. If the level markings are visible on the reservoir, check the level is at least up to the 'minimum' mark.

3 If the fluid does need topping up, wipe around the filler cap and remove it, if not already done, then top up to the correct mark using suitable fluid. If the reservoir has a dipstick, wipe the dipstick, then refit the cap/dipstick, unscrew it again and re-check the fluid level. Make sure you use the correct type of fluid, as there are several different types, and using the wrong one can cause damage to the system.

Power steering fluid

Various types of power steering fluid are used in cars, and most systems use the type of fluid used in automatic transmission systems (of which there are several versions). It's important to check your car's handbook or Haynes Manual for details of the correct type of fluid to use.

4 Refit and tighten the filler cap when you've finished topping up, and wipe up any spills.

If you need to top up regularly, then you'll need to get the car checked at a garage, as it's likely there's a leak. If you notice your steering making a noise when you turn the steering wheel hard, this can indicate that the fluid level is low.

Checking the screenwash fluid

It's an offence and an MoT failure point if the windscreen washers don't work and, obviously, if the reservoir is empty, they won't! It's also potentially dangerous, as well as annoying, to drive without being able to clean the screen.

You can buy premixed screenwash, or concentrate which you mix with water, and both perform the same function, although the concentrate is likely to work out cheaper. In addition to containing cleaning agents to ensure your windscreen sparkles, screen wash also contains a form of antifreeze to stop the washer fluid freezing in cold weather, although if it's minus 12 degrees this might not be effective! Don't be tempted to avoid using screenwash and use plain water, as over time it will go stagnant in the washer bottle, and the smell will be utterly revolting! Plain water won't clean your screen very well either.

With many washer fluid reservoirs, there's no way of telling how full they are, although some may have a dipstick attached to the cap. It's a good idea to top up every week to reduce the chance of running out of fluid.

To check the windscreen wash fluid level, proceed as follows:

1 The screen wash fluid reservoir is often one of the easier things under the bonnet to locate and identify, as it usually has a picture of a windscreen wiper on it. If you're not sure where the reservoir is, check your car's handbook or Haynes Manual.

IF THE SCREENWASH FLUID LEVEL NEEDS TOPPING UP, YOU'LL NEED:

* A clean cloth.
* A small funnel.
* A jug of clean water.
* Screenwash fluid.

2 To top up, simply remove the reservoir cap, which may be a screw or push fit, and fill with washer fluid. You may find a funnel handy. If you're using screenwash concentrate, pour this in first, then top up with tap water to the top of the filler neck.

3 Refit the filler cap when you've finished topping up.

Checks carried out from inside the car

Checking the washers and wipers

To check the front wipers and washers, sit in the car, squirt the washers, and check that they work, then check that the wipers clear the windscreen effectively without smears.

FIXING FAULTY WASHERS

1 If the washer jets are not squirting water on to the windscreen, first of all make sure that there is fluid in the reservoir (in case it's empty!), then listen to see if you can hear a whirring noise from the pump under the bonnet while you're operating

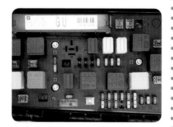

the washers. If not, the pump is probably not working, which could be because of a blown fuse or a fault in the pump itself. You can check the fuse yourself – see the fuse section later in this chapter. If the fuse has not blown, the pump may be faulty.

2 If the pump is working, and the washers are still not squirting, it could be that the washer jets are blocked, or the washer-fluid pipes are disconnected.

3 If you think that the washer jets may be blocked, it's often possible to unblock them using a pin or straightened paperclip. Push it into the small holes in the nozzles a few times, and then operate the washers again to see if water is squirted on to the windscreen.

4 If the washers still don't work, then it's likely that a washer pipe is split, blocked or disconnected. You should be able to check under the bonnet and follow the fluid hose(s) back from the nozzles to see if a hose is leaking or disconnected. If a hose is detached, you might be able to push it back on to its connector.

5 If you've tried all the suggestions, and the pump still isn't working, you may have to take a trip to your local garage for help.

CHECKING A WIPER BLADE

1 If a wiper is smearing, or is squeaking, check the rubber blade. Lift the wiper arm from the windscreen until it locks in the upright position, taking care not to allow it to spring back against the glass, as this could damage the windscreen. If the arm doesn't lock in position, hold it firmly while you check the rubber blade.

2 Wipe the cleaning edge of the blade using a clean cloth that has been dipped in undiluted washer fluid.

3 Run a finger along the edge of the blade to check the rubber for damage. If there are any cracks or splits, a new blade should be fitted.

4 To fit a new blade, first turn the blade at right angles to the arm.

5 Some blades have securing tabs that need to be released before the blade can be removed.

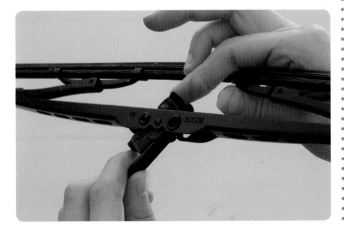

Buying new wiper blades

It's likely to be cheaper to buy wiper blades from a car accessory shop or supermarket, rather than an authorised dealer.

When buying new wiper blades, it's a good idea to take the old ones along, or at least measure them.

Usually, the packaging on new wiper blades will list the models and years of car that the blades will fit. The length of the blades is usually marked on the packaging too, strangely in today's metric world, normally in inches! Make sure that the new blades are the same length as the old ones, noting that often the driver's and passenger's side wiper blades are different lengths.

6 Note which way round the blade fits before removing it, as this will help when fitting the new blade. It may help to take photos before you remove the old blade.

7 Depending on the type of new wiper blade you're fitting, fit the correct adaptor to the blade – check the instructions supplied with the new blade for details. Sometimes you can use the adaptor from the old blade.

8 Fit the new blade to the arm, making sure that it's pushed fully home, then lower the arm gently back on to the windscreen. Check that the wipers work before driving the car. Always squirt washer fluid on to the windscreen before switching on the wipers, as the motor will struggle to move them on a dry windscreen.

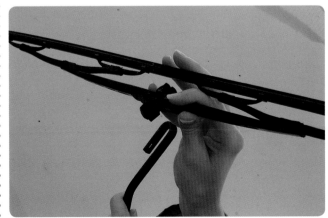

Checks carried out from outside the car

Checking tyres

The wheels and tyres are essential parts of any car, but are often overlooked. It's worth remembering that the only contact the car has with the road is through its tyres, and if they are in poor condition, or incorrectly inflated, it can potentially be very dangerous, affect the car's handling and increase stopping distances. Indeed, faulty tyres contribute to a significant number of accidents each year.

CHECKING TYRE PRESSURES

Checking tyre pressures is a simple and quick job and should be done weekly. In addition to causing excessive tyre wear, driving with incorrectly inflated tyres can reduce fuel economy. The correct pressure will depend on the make and model of car, what size of tyres are fitted, and often what load you're carrying. All the details can usually be found in your car's handbook or Haynes Manual, and the recommended pressures are often given on a sticker at the back edge of one of the front door pillars (visible when you open the door), or sometimes inside the fuel filler flap. It's very important to inflate the tyres to the correct pressure, so if you're in any doubt, contact your vehicle manufacturer or a tyre specialist, and make a note of the recommended pressures, which will be given in PSI (pounds per square inch) or 'bar'. Note that in most cases, the pressures for the front and rear tyres will be different.

To check the pressures, proceed as follows:

1 Ideally, you should check the tyre pressures with the tyres cold – before driving the car, not after. If you have to check the pressures after driving, or during a journey, make sure that you re-check them afterwards when the tyres are cold. There can be a significant difference between hot and cold tyre pressures.

2 Firstly, remove the dust cap from the tyre valve. If this is missing, it's no great cause for concern. It doesn't keep the air in, it merely keeps the valve clean and protects it from damage, although it's always a good idea to replace a missing cap.

TO CHECK THE TYRES, YOU WILL NEED:

* A tyre-pressure gauge.
* A tyre pump (foot pump or electric compressor/pump).
* A tyre tread-depth gauge.

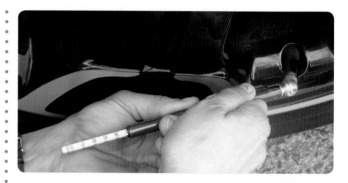

3 Next, firmly press the nozzle of the pressure gauge on to the valve, make sure that the air is not leaking out of the connection between the tyre valve and gauge, and take a reading. Refer to the panel on tyre pressure gauges for details of the different types available.

4 If the pressure is too low, use the air pump at a petrol station, a foot pump, or a mini compressor, to add air for a few seconds.

5 Re-check the pressure, and continue to add air until the correct reading is shown on the gauge. Don't worry if you add too much air, it's easy to remove – simply use a ballpoint pen, or similar small implement, to press the pin in the middle of the valve to release a small quantity of air at a time.

6 At some petrol stations there's an inflation machine, which will automatically add the correct quantity of air once you've set the correct pressure on a meter.

7 Once you have the correct pressure, refit the dust cap.

8 Be aware that many filling stations charge by the minute to check and fill your tyres. To speed things up a bit, you can remove all the valve caps before putting money in the slot, and treat the check as an F1 pit stop!

9 If you regularly need to top up a tyre, it's likely that there's a slow puncture, which could be caused by a leaking valve, a small hole in the tyre, or a poor seal where the tyre fits on the wheel. Whatever the cause, it's a good idea to get the tyre fixed as soon as possible.

CHECKING TYRE TREAD DEPTH

Whenever you check tyre pressures, it's also a good idea to keep an eye on the depth of tread left on the tyres. The legal limit for tread depth in the UK is 1.6mm over the central ¾ of the tyre – this means that the edges can actually be bald! It's really not a good idea to allow the tyres to wear this far, and it's sensible to change a tyre once any part of the tread wears below 3mm.

1 It's easy to check the tread depth using an inexpensive gauge or, at a push, the raised edge of a 20-pence coin.

2 To check the depth, insert the inner prong of the gauge (or 20-pence coin) into the tread of the tyre and take a reading. It's a good idea to take a reading over several different parts of the tyre to see if they vary much – if they do, it's a good indication that something is amiss, possibly a steering or suspension problem, or incorrect tyre pressure.

Tyre pressure gauges

Several different types of tyre pressure gauge are available, and most foot pumps and electric compressors have a pressure gauge built in. Generally, it's best to buy a separate gauge for checking the pressure – the main types are:

* A simple 'slider bar' gauge.
* A dial gauge.
* A digital gauge.

Each type has its pros and cons, and generally, as with all tools, you get what you pay for. A good-quality dial gauge is perhaps the most reliable type, and the better gauges have an air-release button for allowing air out of the tyre if you overinflate it.

The most important thing to remember is that different types of gauges (or even two examples of the same type of gauge) may give slightly different readings, so always use the same gauge to check your tyres.

3 As a general rule, if tyres are worn more on one edge than the other, the wheel alignment needs checking; if they are worn more in the middle, the tyre has been overinflated; if they are worn on both outer edges, it has been underinflated.

4 In addition to weekly pressure and tread-depth checks, you should also check the general condition of the tyre. Look for bulges, cracks, cuts and perishing in the tread and on the sides of the tyre (the 'tyre sidewall'). Also check the condition of the wheel itself, looking to see if it's bent or damaged. Visit your local tyre specialist for advice if you find any problems.

Tyre size markings

So, what do all those confusing numbers and letters marked on the tyre mean, such as '185/70 R 13 87T'? These markings indicate the exact specification of the tyre, and the meanings of the various markings in the example given are as follows:

185 indicates the width of the tyre in mm.

70 indicates the ratio of the tyre section's height to its width, expressed as a percentage. If no number is present at this point the ratio is considered to be 'standard', which is 82 per cent.

R indicates the tyre is of radial-ply construction (older tyres used a 'cross-ply' construction).

13 indicates the wheel diameter for the tyre is 13 inches.

87 is an index number that indicates the maximum load the tyre can carry at its maximum recommended speed.

T represents the maximum permitted speed for the tyre, which should be at least 6 per cent higher than the car's maximum possible speed.

It doesn't help that there's a mixture of metric and imperial measurements, along with a percentage chucked in for good measure! The tyre specification markings always appear around the edge of the tyre, and you should be able to recognise them from the example below. You'll need to know the tyre size when looking for the recommended pressure, and also if you need to order a new tyre.

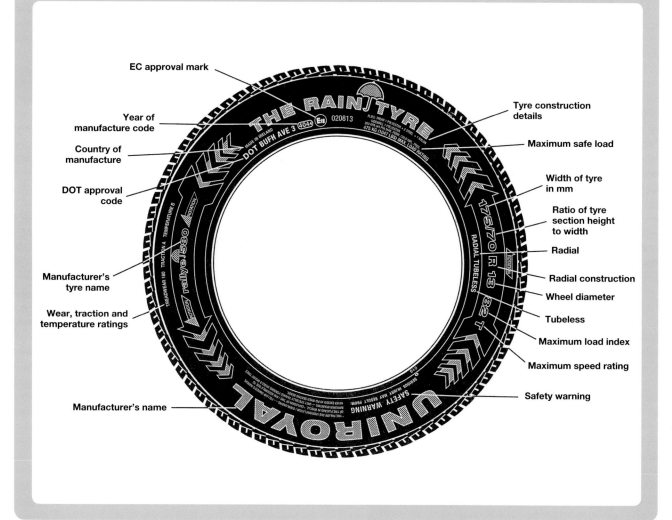

EC approval mark

Year of manufacture code

Country of manufacture

DOT approval code

Manufacturer's tyre name

Wear, traction and temperature ratings

Manufacturer's name

Tyre construction details

Maximum safe load

Width of tyre in mm

Ratio of tyre section height to width

Radial

Radial construction

Wheel diameter

Tubeless

Maximum load index

Maximum speed rating

Safety warning

Checking light bulbs

Once a week, when you're carrying out the other checks, it's a good idea to walk around the car and check all the light bulbs. A failed bulb can be a reason for the police to stop your car, and can also be dangerous.

You can find details of how to check the bulbs in Chapter 5.

RENEWING A BULB

Although it should really be a simple job to renew a bulb, that's not always the case on a modern car. Bulb renewal can still be straightforward on many cars, but on certain models, to change a headlight bulb it's necessary to remove the front bumper or the entire light unit! On other cars, the front wheel needs to be removed, and the bulbs can then be accessed via a flap in the wheel-arch liner. These operations can take an experienced mechanic with a vehicle lift and the correct tools over an hour, so it's likely to prove a challenge for a DIY mechanic trying to change a bulb on their driveway with just a screwdriver!

On the plus side, many manufacturers have designed their cars so that changing a bulb is a relatively simple task. Over the following few pages, you will find examples explaining how to renew the most common types of bulbs.

A vast range of different types of bulbs may be fitted, and when you need a new bulb, the only way to be sure that you're buying the correct new bulb is to take the old bulb along with you when buying the new one.

It would be impossible to cover the procedure for changing every bulb for every car in this book, but a few examples for renewing the major bulbs on various cars are included in the following section to give you an idea of what may be involved. Your car's handbook or Haynes Manual will guide you through the procedures for your particular car if you need further help.

CITROËN DS3 FRONT INDICATOR BULB
Passenger's side front indicator bulb

1 Open the bonnet, and look for the back of the indicator bulb holder, at the front of the engine compartment.

2 Grasp the plastic tabs on the back of the bulb holder, and twist the bulb holder anticlockwise until it can be removed from the light unit.

3 With the bulb holder removed, carefully push and twist the bulb anticlockwise to release it from the bulb holder. Note that the bulb is orange-coloured, and the light lens is clear.

4 Fit the new bulb, pushing and twisting it clockwise until it locks in position. Check that the new bulb works before you twist the bulb holder back into position!

Spare bulb kit

You can buy a set of spare bulbs for your car, which can be kept in the glove box or boot. Note that when driving in some foreign countries, it's compulsory to carry a set of suitable spare bulbs.

You will usually be able to buy spare bulb kits from an official dealership, or any car accessory shop or motor factor, but you'll need to make sure that you buy a suitable set for your specific model of car.

A spare bulb kit will not contain every type of bulb you need for your car, but it will include the main ones that you might need in an emergency – headlight bulb, sidelight bulb, indicator bulbs, tail-light bulb and brake light bulb. The kit will also usually contain a selection of spare fuses.

Note that sometimes red- and amber-coloured bulbs may be used for the indicators and rear lights where the lens itself is clear.

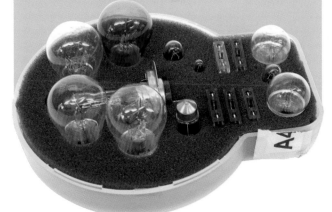

CITROËN DS3 HEADLIGHT BULB

Changing a headlight bulb on a Citroën DS3 is fairly typical of many cars, and quite straightforward. In fact women have a bit of an advantage, as they tend to have smaller hands, and the lack of space to reach the bulbs is the biggest problem. It's a good idea to use a mirror and a torch to look at how the bulb is fixed first. It's also a good idea to take pictures as you go along, as a guide to help you put everything back together!

Passenger's side main-beam headlight bulb
To renew the passenger's side main-beam bulb, proceed as follows:

1 Open the bonnet.

2 Working at the back of the light, carefully pull the rubber dust cover from the back of the light.

3 Lift the rubber cover away, and you should be able to see the headlight bulb and its wiring plug and retaining clip.

4 Carefully pull the wiring plug from the tab on the back of the bulb.

5 Release bulb retaining clip. This is a wire spring clip that holds the bulb in place in the back of the light housing. To release the clip you need to press the two ends of the clip (at the top of the light) towards each other until the clip springs free from the tabs in the light and hinges down.

6 Carefully lift the bulb from the rear of the light. Note how the bulb locates in the housing so that you can fit the new bulb the correct way up.

7 Fit the new bulb, taking care not to touch the glass. Make sure it's located correctly – there's a tab on top of the bulb's metal base that sits in a slot in the light housing.

8 Flip the bulb clip up and clip it in position in the housing to secure the bulb – this can be quite awkward to do.

9 Carefully push the wiring connector on to the tab on the new bulb, then check that the light works!

10 Push the dust cover into position.

VAUXHALL VECTRA DIRECTION INDICATOR SIDE REPEATER BULB

Driver's side indicator side repeater bulb

1 Stick some masking or place a piece of card on the wing just behind the lens to protect the paintwork.

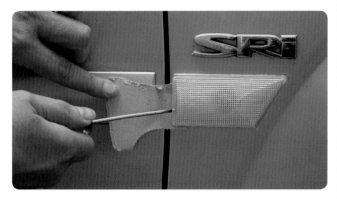

2 Using a small screwdriver, carefully prise the back of the lens towards the front of the car and outwards, and it should pop out.

3 Twist the bulb holder anticlockwise and pull it from the back of the light.

4 Fit a new bulb, and check it works!

5 Fit the bulb holder to the light, then place the front of the light back in the hole in the wing, and give the rear end of the lens a firm press – it should pop back in easily.

VAUXHALL VECTRA REAR NUMBER PLATE LIGHT BULB

1 Using a small screwdriver, carefully press the light unit retaining tab, and pull the light unit from the bumper.

2 Twist the bulb holder anticlockwise to release it from the light unit.

3 Pull the bulb from the bulb holder.

4 Push the new bulb into the bulb holder, push the bulb holder into position and twist it clockwise to secure it, then carefully push the light unit into position in the bumper.

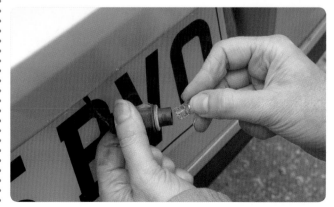

CITROËN DS3 REAR BULBS

On some cars, you need to remove the rear light cluster to be able to change the rear bulbs, such as tail-light and brake-light bulbs. A good example of a car where this is necessary is the Citroën DS3.

Brake/tail-light bulb

1 Open the tailgate, and pull out the plastic cover from the rear corner of the boot for access to the light-securing screw.

2 Pull back the sound insulation to expose the wiring plug and the light-securing screw.

3 Reach in through the hole in the corner of the boot, and disconnect the wiring plug.

4 Support the light unit from outside the boot, then unscrew the light-securing screw.

5 You should now be able to carefully lift the light unit from the rear corner of the car.

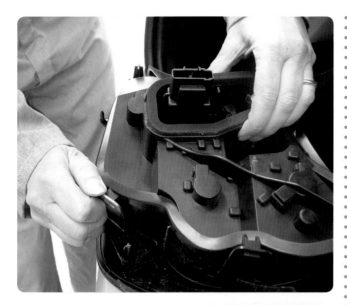

6 Now you need to carefully ease back the plastic tabs securing the bulb holder assembly to the back of the light unit – there are four tabs spaced out around the bulb holder.

7 Lift the bulb holder from the rear of the light unit for access to the bulbs.

8 To remove a bulb, carefully push and twist it anti-clockwise to release if from the bulb holder.

9 Fit the new bulb, by gently pushing it in to the bulb holder and twisting the bulb clockwise to secure it in position.

10 It's now a good idea to temporarily reconnect the wiring plug to the back of the bulb holder to check that the new bulb works.

11 Disconnect the wiring plug again, if necessary, then clip the bulb holder in to position in the light unit, and carefully place the light unit in to position against the body, taking care not to scratch the paint.

12 Working inside the boot, refit the light-securing screw, then reconnect the wiring plug, push the sound insulation back in to position, and refit the plastic access panel.

If you find that a light isn't working properly, and fitting a new bulb doesn't solve the problem, the most likely cause is a bad electrical connection. The electricity flows back to the battery through the metal body of the car, and if the flow of electricity to a bulb is interrupted, the light won't work.

Corrosion prevents electricity from flowing, and is a common cause of problems. Check the wiring connectors for corrosion, and also check the contacts inside the bulb holder. Even if water hasn't got in, condensation can often cause the metal to rust. If you find any corrosion, clean the affected area with abrasive paper or a small wire brush, then spray the components with water dispersant (such as WD-40). In the worst cases you might have to replace the affected parts.

If there's no trace of corrosion, check the earth connections for the light. Usually, there's an earth wire running from the light unit to a screw on a nearby body panel, or the earth wire may be plugged into an earth connector block attached to the car's body. Check that the earth connections to the body are not corroded, and that they're tight. If a connection is bolted to a body panel, unscrew the bolt and try cleaning the area around the bolt with abrasive paper or a small wire brush. Reconnect the earth wire and tighten the bolt, then spray the components with water dispersant.

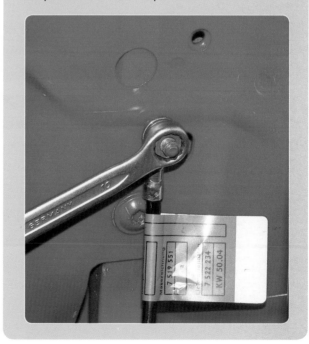

Checking and renewing fuses

Fuses are fitted in an electrical circuit as a safety device, and are designed to break when too much current flows through them, in order to prevent damage to electrical components and, in the worst case, dangerous overheating. If you notice that an electrical item is not working on your car – or sometimes several items, as often one fuse protects several circuits – the first thing to check is the fuse for the particular faulty circuit.

Your car's handbook or Haynes Manual will usually tell you which fuses protect which circuits, and also where to find the fuses. Fuses are normally housed in a fuse box or, on many cars, several fuse boxes, which may be located in or under the glove box, in a compartment near the driver's right knee, or under the bonnet itself. Often, the fuses will be numbered, either with numbers stamped into the fuse box, or printed on a sticker on the fuse box lid.

You can recognise a blown fuse easily, because the wire in the fuse will be broken if it has blown – see the accompanying photo for an example of how a blown fuse looks when compared to a new one. Changing a fuse is a simple process, as follows:

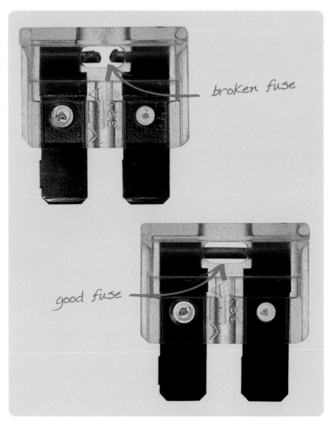

broken fuse

good fuse

1 Simply pull the fuse from the terminals in the fuse box. On some cars you'll find a plastic tool for removing the fuses clipped into the fuse box or its lid.

2 The new fuse must be of the same rating as the old one. It should be the same colour, or have the same number (5, 10, 15, 20, 25, 30, etc.) stamped on it.

3 Push the new fuse firmly into its slot in the fuse box, making sure that the contacts on the fuse slide fully into the terminals in the fuse box.

4 Switch on the appropriate circuit – if the new fuse blows, there's a problem, and you should find the cause of the problem or seek advice before fitting another fuse.

Latches and hinges

There are many latches and hinges on your car, all of which will benefit from regular maintenance. If you've noticed creaking, groaning or clicking noises when you open a door, this is likely to be caused by a lack of lubrication to a hinge. More frustratingly, a poorly maintained latch can fail to work, leaving you with a door, boot or bonnet that stubbornly refuses to open!

To keep your latches and hinges in good, noise-free working condition will only take a few minutes every three months or so, and the only tool you will need is a can of spray grease.

The best lubricant to buy is an aerosol white lithium spray grease. This is inexpensive and readily available at motoring outlets, petrol stations and a number of online retailers. The benefits of lithium grease are that it's water and heat resistant, non-hardening, long lasting and it also helps to prevent rust. The grease should come with a small straw-type applicator, which you can attach to the nozzle of the can, making even the hardest-to-reach areas accessible. A can should last a number of years.

The doors on your car will normally have two hinges and a 'check strap' at the front, which keeps the door open. It will also have a latch at the rear,

which keeps it closed until you operate the door handle to open it. The rear tailgate or boot and the bonnet will also have latches and hinges. All of these require regular greasing, which is a simple and quick job.

With the door, tailgate, boot or bonnet fully open, aim the can at the hinge, check strap or latch, and press the button for a second or so. Use a soft cloth to wipe away any overspray. Repeat this procedure on the other hinges, check straps and latches.

SERVICING

Servicing your car regularly is important for safety and reliability, and can save on costly bills. The manufacturers intend your car to be serviced according to their recommended schedule in order to maintain its performance and prolong its life, and it's vital to follow the service schedule if your car is under warranty in order to prevent the warranty from becoming void.

There are a number of different levels of service, from the basic to the 'all singing, all dancing!' Which one your car requires will depend on how many miles it has covered, the time that has passed since the last service, and your vehicle manufacturer's recommendations. This chapter explains what happens during servicing, what gets checked and renewed, and what you can do for yourself to save money and learn more about your car.

Service schedules

Every car manufacturer specifies a service schedule for each of its models, and it's important to make sure that this schedule is followed. If servicing is neglected, or worse still ignored, it's almost inevitable that sooner or later your car will suffer the consequences, which could prove inconvenient, expensive, or both! In some cases, a lack of maintenance can also mean that potentially dangerous faults go undetected.

If you have the service record book that was originally supplied with your car when it was new, this will usually contain a service schedule. Often, the service schedule is also given in the car's handbook, but if you don't have a service schedule, an authorised dealer for your make of car should be able to provide one. You'll also find a service schedule, and details of all the servicing procedures, in the Haynes Manual for your car.

The intervals between services are determined by either time or mileage. This is because some items, such as engine oil for example, deteriorate with time as well as the mileage covered. Usually, there will be a number of different service schedules for a particular car, and which one is applicable will depend on the mileage covered, the time since the last service, and how old the car is. The procedures that need to be carried out at each service will vary according to the service schedule – for instance the engine oil and filter will probably need to be changed at every service, but the brake fluid will only need to be changed perhaps every two years, or after a relatively high mileage (bake fluid deteriorates with age). Most cars will require at least a basic service every year or 18,000 miles – sometimes more often.

Manufacturers and garages will often give the various levels of service different names, or sometimes numbers. Many garages will also provide you with a 'tick sheet' showing which checks and procedures have been carried out on the car. The tick sheet may be provided by the garage, by the car manufacturer, or may be one

provided by a voluntary industry scheme such as the Good Garage Scheme.

Below is an example service checklist for a full service. Many of the operations have been covered already in Chapter 3, or are covered later in this chapter, and some, such as fitting seat covers so the mechanic doesn't make your seat dirty, are self-explanatory – but for those which are not, the tasks are best left to somebody experienced, or to a professional mechanic.

Service check list

* Renew engine oil (see pages 56–59).
* Renew oil filter (see pages 56–59).
* Check and if necessary top up screen wash fluid (see page 37).
* Check windscreen washers and wipers (see pages 38–39).
* Check coolant level (see page 34).
* Check cooling system, including fan operation.
* Check and record antifreeze strength.
* Check level and condition of brake fluid (see page 35).
* Check horn.
* Check power steering operation and fluid level/condition (see page 36).
* Check fuel lines.
* Check brake pipes.
* Check condition and security of exhaust.
* Check all steering joints, mountings and gaiters.
* Check all suspension joints, mountings and gaiters.
* Check tyre condition and pressures (see pages 40–41).
* Check drive shaft joints and gaiters.
* Check wheel bearings.
* Check operation and condition of brakes, including handbrake.
* Check operation of air bag light (where applicable).
* Check timing belt replacement interval.

The MoT test

Many people confuse the MoT test with a service, however the two are actually very different. An MoT test is a legal requirement, and is a basic test of the car's safety according to government guidelines. As you'll see in the next chapter, the MoT isn't particularly comprehensive in terms of the items that get checked, and no maintenance work is carried out as part of the test.

✳ Check operation of ABS (Anti-lock Braking System) light (where applicable).

✳ Check operation of all interior and exterior lights (see pages 43–47).

✳ Check for damage to bodywork, lights and trim.

✳ Road test and report any findings.

✳ Re-set service indicator.

✳ Stamp service book.

✳ Renew air filter (see page 60).

✳ Renew spark plugs (petrol engine) (see page 62).

✳ Renew fuel filter.

✳ Check and if necessary top up gearbox oil level.

✳ Check clutch cable/cylinder (where applicable).

✳ Grease all greasing points (where applicable).

✳ Check throttle body.

✳ Check battery condition and apply protector spray to terminals (see page 78).

✳ Check vacuum pipes.

✳ Check engine breather system.

✳ Check all auxiliary drive belts.

✳ Check fuel filler cap.

✳ Lubricate all door hinges, locks and catches (see page 49).

✳ Check operation of suspension dampers.

✳ Check air conditioning operation (where applicable), and check for bad odour.

✳ Check condition and operation of all seatbelts.

✳ Replace pollen filter (see page 61).

✳ Carry out engine diagnostic health check.

The most basic level of service may be called an 'interim' service, 'small' service, 'bronze' service, 'level 1' service, or similar. This will usually include basic checks, and changing the engine oil and oil filter. Oil is vital to your engine, and over time it becomes dirty and breaks down, reducing its effectiveness in protecting your engine. The oil filter collects debris from the oil and gets clogged up over time, so it's vital to renew it at the same time as changing the engine oil. This service will usually be carried out once a year – more often if you cover a high mileage.

Moving on to the next, usually more comprehensive, level of service, you might find it referred to as an 'annual' service, 'standard' service, 'silver' service, or 'level 2' service. This will usually include more checks and procedures than a basic service, and may involve renewing items such as the air filter or fuel filter.

The most comprehensive level of service is often called a 'full' service, 'gold' or 'platinum' service, or a 'level 3' service. This is usually only carried out every two or or three years, or after a certain mileage has been reached, such as 40,000.

In addition, other major operations, such as timing belt ('cam belt') renewal (not applicable to all cars), coolant change or brake fluid change, will be given specific mileage/time intervals.

Don't get too hung up on the terminology used to refer to the service levels ('interim', 'level 2', 'silver', etc) – the important thing is to find out the specific service schedules recommended by the manufacturer for your particular car.

Here is an example of a manufacturer's service schedule. As previously stated it is important to ensure your garage adheres to the service schedule for your particular vehicle.

DIY servicing

Although it's unlikely that you'll be able to carry out all the jobs required for every service schedule, many of the servicing operations are easy to perform, and will be well within your capabilities. Over the next few pages example procedures are included for engine oil and filter renewal, air filter renewal, pollen filter renewal, and changing spark plugs, along with basic details of some of the other operations that can be part of a service.

Buying parts

If you plan to service your car, you will need to buy parts, oil, and possibly other fluids. There are a number of places you can buy these items. To be sure of obtaining the correct parts, you'll need to know the model and year of manufacture of your car, although it's often possible to buy just by quoting your registration number, or the VIN (Vehicle Identification Number), which is unique to every car, and can be found on your car's registration document.

Authorised dealers – This is the only place you should buy parts if your car is still under warranty. You'll generally pay more for parts at an authorised dealer, but at least you can be pretty sure that the parts are the correct ones.

Accessory shops – These are good for servicing components. Filters and spark plugs, etc, bought from a good car accessory shop are usually of the same standard as those used by the car manufacturer. Most of these shops also sell tools and general accessories. Some have parts counters where components needed for almost any servicing or repair job can be bought or ordered.

Motor factors – Good factors will stock all the more important servicing components. Prices are likely to be competitive, as most motor factors also sell components to the garage trade.

Other sources of parts – Beware of parts or materials bought from market stalls, car boot sales, auction websites, etc. These items aren't necessarily sub-standard, but there's little chance of compensation if they are unsatisfactory. Although it's possible to obtain some bargains, be sure that you're buying components of reasonable quality, and beware of counterfeit products.

Even if you never wish to attempt any of them, it can be handy to know what your garage should be doing and how they should be doing it! Bear in mind that the procedures described are only typical example procedures, and the details and procedures for your car may differ from those shown here. For full details of the procedures for your specific car, refer to the relevant Haynes Manual.

Safety

If you're going to carry out any work on your car, the first priority must always be safety.

* Never take any unnecessary risks, and always try to use the correct tools for the job you're doing – don't try to improvise.
* Ensure you follow the correct procedure for performing a task – details will be given in the Haynes Manual for your specific car.
* It's a sensible precaution to wear disposable gloves whenever you're working on a car, as this will protect your hands and will also make it a lot easier to clean them afterwards. For certain jobs it's also a good idea to wear eye protection.
* Remove any jewellery and clothing which might become caught, eg, long necklaces and scarves, and similarly take care if you have long hair.
* Bear in mind that if you're working under the bonnet and the engine has run recently, various engine components, particularly the exhaust system, can be hot enough to cause serious burns.
* If you're working under the bonnet with the engine running, keep well clear of the moving components.
* Be careful where you put tools when you're not using them – they can easily slip into inaccessible locations, and on some cars it's very easy to accidentally short-out the battery terminals with metal tools, which can cause damage, and possibly a fire.

Safely raising your car

For some procedures on your car, it will be necessary to raise the car off the ground. It may sometimes be necessary to raise the car to drain the engine oil, as it may be very difficult to reach the oil drain plug with the car resting on its wheels.

Never support the car using just a jack (even a 'professional' trolley jack), as if the jack fails, the car will drop, possibly causing serious injury to anybody working under it.

Always ensure that the car is on level ground before attempting to jack it up – never lift the car if it's parked on sloping ground.

Once the car has been raised using a jack, to ensure that the car is safely supported, you can use axle stands, or ramps.

USING RAMPS

1. Make sure that the ramps are in good condition and are suitable for the weight of your car.

2. Park the car on level ground, then place the ramps against the tyres, and line them up with the wheels so that you can drive on to them in a straight line.

3. Ask a friend or relative to keep an eye on things as you drive on to the ramps, just in case the ramps move, or the car is not lined up correctly.

4. Drive very slowly on to the ramps, and once the car is safely in position, apply the handbrake and stop the engine.

5. For safety, chock the wheels that are resting on the ground.

6. When you drive off the ramps, make sure that all's clear in the direction you're going to be moving, and be prepared to apply the brakes gently as the car rolls down from the ramps.

USING A JACK AND AXLE STANDS

1. Make sure that the handbrake is applied, and use wooden blocks or suitable large stones to chock any wheels that are not going to be raised.

2. It's very important to make sure that you only place a jack under the proper reinforced jacking points specified by the manufacturer. If you place the jack anywhere else, it's likely that you will damage the car. To find the locations of the jacking points and recommended axle-stand positions, refer to your car's handbook or the Haynes Manual. Normally, you should place a block of wood between the top of the jack and the car jacking point. Always follow the jack manufacturer's instructions when using the jack.

3. Move the jack into position under the relevant corner of the car, then raise the jack to lift the car to the required height, and place an axle stand under the recommended support point.

4. Gently lower the jack until the weight of the car is supported by the axle stand.

5. If you need to raise one of the other corners of the car at the same time, repeat the procedure at the other corner, again making sure that you place the jack and axle stand in the recommended positions.

6. When you've finished carrying out the work, lower the car by again placing the jack under the relevant jacking point, and raising the car until the axle stand can be pulled out. Lower the jack gently until the wheel and tyre are supporting the car.

Servicing procedures

Engine oil and oil filter renewal

The old engine oil is removed from the engine by unscrewing a drain plug from the 'sump' underneath the engine.

On many cars it will be necessary to remove a plastic shield, or undertray, from under the engine compartment for access to the drain plug. Often this can be more time-consuming than draining the oil!

The type of drain plug fitted depends on the make of car – you may be able to unscrew it with a spanner, or you may need a special key that you can use with a ratchet and socket set. Make sure that you use the correct tool, and never try to do the job with a tool that doesn't fit, as you may damage the drain plug, the tool, or yourself! If you're not sure about the type of tool you need, consult the Haynes Manual for your car (or ask the staff at your local car accessory shop, who should be able to help), which will also provide you with all the correct information for renewing the oil on your specific car. The following step-by-step guide gives a generic guide to a typical oil renewal procedure, so that you know what to expect.

TOOLS AND EQUIPMENT REQUIRED

* A 5-litre can of the correct oil for your car – consult the owner's handbook or Haynes Manual for details.
* A container to place under the engine to catch the old engine oil – make sure that it will fit under your engine, and will hold at least 6 litres of fluid to avoid any risk of it overflowing.
* A small plastic funnel for filling the engine with fresh oil.
* Plenty of clean cloths.
* A new oil filter and a new oil drain plug sealing ring to suit your specific car – your parts supplier will be able to advise on the correct parts.
* Suitable tools to remove the engine undertray, where applicable.
* A suitable spanner or suitable key to fit the oil drain plug.
* Depending on the type of oil filter fitted to your car, you may need an oil-filter removal tool.
* Your Haynes Manual!

TO RENEW THE ENGINE OIL AND FILTER:

1 Take your car for a drive, or start the engine and leave it running until the engine reaches its normal operating temperature. Once the engine is up to operating temperature, stop the engine and remove the ignition key, so that you're not tempted to accidentally start the engine with no oil in it! From this point on, beware when working on the car, as the engine and surrounding components will be hot!

2 Open the bonnet, then put on a pair of disposable gloves, and remove the oil filler cap from the top of the engine.

3 Have a look under the engine to see if a plastic undertray is fitted, which you may need to remove to reach the oil drain plug. On some cars, you can just remove a small access panel from the undertray for access to the plug, or you may find that no undertray is fitted. On cars with an undertray, have a look to see how it's secured – it will normally be fastened with small screws or plastic clips. At this point you will need to decide whether you need to jack up the car to allow access to the undertray and drain plug. If you do, refer to 'Safely raising your car' on page 55.

4 Once you've removed the undertray, find the oil drain plug. The drain plug will be very near the bottom of the sump (the lowest part of the engine) and will either be screwed into the bottom face of the sump, or may be screwed into the side or rear of the sump on some cars.

5 Place the draining container under the sump drain plug, making sure that the oil will drain into the container, then slacken the drain plug using a spanner or the special key. The plug may be very stiff to start with, so take care not to catch your hands on the engine if it suddenly moves!

6 Once the drain plug has been slackened, try to unscrew it by hand, or very slowly with the spanner or tool. As the plug slackens off, oil will begin to come out around its sides. Try to unscrew the plug by hand for the final few turns, keeping it pressed into the sump, and get ready to pull your hand, and the drain plug,

swiftly away once the plug is fully unscrewed. Remember that the engine and the oil will be hot, so pull your hand away quickly to avoid the oil running down your sleeve. The oil will come out with some force to start with, and the flow of oil will gradually slow to a trickle, although this may take some time. As a very rough guide, you will probably need to leave the oil to drain for around 10 minutes.

7 While the oil is draining, wipe the drain plug with a clean cloth, and remove the sealing ring. Sometimes the sealing ring may stick to the sump, but usually it will come off with the drain plug. The sealing ring may be made of metal, plastic or rubber, depending on the type of car. Clean the drain plug thoroughly, and fit it with a new sealing ring of the correct type.

8 When the oil stops draining, or the flow has reduced to a few drips, wipe around the drain-plug hole, then screw in the plug, by hand, and tighten it using the spanner or key. Make sure that the plug is tight, but take care not to over-tighten it, as this could cause problems next time the oil is drained.

9 Now you need to find the oil filter. This will be either a cylindrical metal canister near the bottom of the engine, either at the back, front, or side or, increasingly, a housing with a plastic cover, usually near the top of the engine, containing a paper element.

10 Reposition the draining container underneath the oil filter then, if you have a metal canister-type oil filter, use the oil filter removal tool to slacken the filter (turn it anticlockwise), remembering it may be hot, so you may need a cloth to protect your hands. It may be very tight at first.

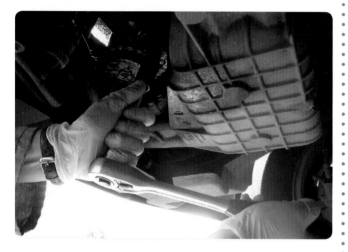

11 If you have a paper-element-type filter, the cover can usually be unscrewed using a suitable spanner or socket. Often, the paper-element filter will be clipped to the cover.

12 Once the filter is loose, remove it by hand. Drain the oil from inside the filter into the container. When you remove the filter from the engine, the oil will probably run down the side of the engine, so be prepared – it's a good idea to place some old cloths or newspaper under the engine to catch any spills.

13 If your car has a metal-canister filter, wipe clean around the filter mounting on the engine, using a clean cloth. Take the

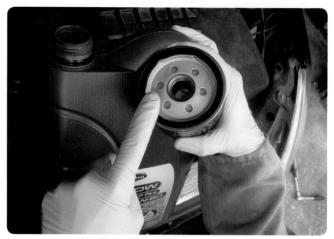

new oil filter and, using your finger, smear a little clean engine oil on the rubber sealing ring, then screw the new filter on to the engine by hand until the sealing ring touches the engine. Tighten the filter by hand about another half- to three-quarters of a turn – don't use any tools to tighten the filter. Pull the draining container and tools out from under the car.

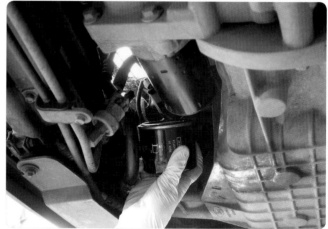

14 If your car has a paper-element filter, clean the housing and cover, and fit the new filter. On some cars you will need to renew the rubber sealing ring fitted to the cover – usually a thin 'O-ring' fitted in a groove around the edge of the cover. You can usually remove the old sealing ring with a thin screwdriver, and then fit the new one by hand. Screw the filter cover on to the housing, taking care not to over-tighten it.

15 Where applicable, refit the plastic undertray under the engine then, if you had to jack the car up to drain the oil and remove the filter, now is the time to lower it back to the ground.

16 Check you car's handbook, or the Haynes Manual, to see how much oil the engine needs, then pour in about two-thirds of the recommended quantity through the filler hole at the top of the engine. Pour the oil in slowly, and use a funnel to stop spills.

17 Wait a few minutes for the oil to drain down into the engine, then pull out the dipstick, wipe it clean, then re-insert it and check the oil level – see pages 32–33.

18 Keep topping up the oil and re-checking the level until the level reaches the upper mark on the dipstick, then refit the filler cap and check that the dipstick is pushed firmly in.

19 Start the engine. The red oil pressure warning light on the dashboard may take a few seconds to go out – if it doesn't go out, stop the engine! Run the engine for a few minutes,

and check for leaks around the oil filter and drain plug. Re-tighten slightly if necessary, but don't over-tighten.

20 Stop the engine and wait a few minutes for the oil to run down into the engine again, then re-check the oil level. Top up if necessary, but don't overfill. Pour the old oil into a container with a lid (an old five-litre oil container is ideal) and take it to your local oil-recycling centre. Most waste disposal sites and most garages have a waste-oil tank, and will probably take the oil for you if you ask. Don't pour it down a drain or into the ground!

21 That's the job completed – you've changed the oil and filter.

Air filter renewal

TOOLS AND EQUIPMENT REQUIRED

* Suitable screwdriver(s) to slacken air filter cover clips and/or screws.
* Clean cloth.
* New air filter of the correct type for your car.

Most manufacturers recommend that the air filter is changed around every two years or 20,000 miles. Often, by this point, the filter has become clogged, so you might want to change it more regularly.

The filter stops dirt, dust and insects from being sucked into the engine. If the filter is very dirty or blocked, the engine won't run efficiently, may lack performance, and the fuel consumption might be higher than normal. The filter is normally a paper element.

Air filters are usually housed in a rectangular plastic casing next to the engine, or a round casing on top of the engine – check your car's handbook or Haynes Manual if you're not sure of the filter's location. Sometimes you may have to unclip or disconnect a hose or wiring plug before you can remove the air filter cover.

TO RENEW A TYPICAL AIR FILTER:

1 Check around the air filter cover to see if any wiring plugs or hoses need to be disconnected to allow the cover to be lifted off. If necessary, disconnect the hose(s) and plug(s).

2 Release the clips and/or unscrew the securing screws, then lift the cover from the air filter housing.

3 Lift out the air filter, noting which way up it's fitted (some filters fit either way up). Make sure that the new filter is the same as the one you've taken out.

4 Wipe out the casing and the cover using a clean cloth. Be careful not to get any dirt or dust into the air intake that passes air from the filter to the engine.

5 Fit the new filter into the housing, making sure that it's the right way up, then refit the cover and secure it with the clips and/or screws.

6 If you had to disconnect any hoses or wiring plugs to remove the filter, don't forget to reconnect them when you've finished.

Cabin or 'pollen' filter renewal

These filters were introduced to cars a number of years ago to filter the dust and pollen that would otherwise enter the car via the fresh air and heater vents. A cabin filter is usually a pleated paper element, very similar in appearance to an engine air filter. However, they are not fitted to every car, so check your car's handbook or Haynes Manual before you spend ages looking, as they can be particularly difficult to locate!

Some manufacturers have a tendency to hide cabin filters in obscure places, such as behind the glove box, or under the front scuttle panel (that's the plastic panel that sits under your windscreen wiper blades). Often, access can be tricky, and several items need to be removed, which is possibly why so many cars have cabin filters that are filthy and have quite obviously not been changed for years!

It's very important to change the filter regularly though, as a clogged or dirty cabin filter can greatly reduce the effectiveness of the car's ventilation system, and the air conditioning system, if fitted. A clogged cabin filter can also introduce allergens into the car, which is bad news for asthma sufferers, although none of us should be breathing dirty air!

Cabin filter renewal may not always be a quick job, but in most cases it shouldn't be difficult. Your car's handbook or Haynes Manual should give details of the location of the filter and how to renew it.

Here's a typical example showing the details for a Vauxhall Vectra – this one is quite easy:

1 Open the bonnet, then carefully pull the rubber seal from the scuttle panel at the back of the engine compartment.

2 Lift up the plastic cover to reveal the cabin filter.

3 Carefully pull up the plastic retaining tabs on the top corners of the filter.

4 Lift the filter up and out from its housing.

5 Slide the new filter into position in the housing, taking care not to bend it, and making sure that it slides correctly into place. On some filters there are airflow direction arrows, so make sure they point in the right direction (the air flows from the engine compartment through the filter to the ventilation system inside the car).

6 Push the two retaining tabs down to secure the filter, then lower the plastic cover into position and refit the rubber seal, making sure that it's correctly located on the scuttle panel.

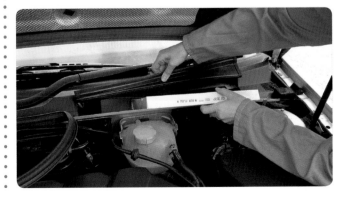

Spark plug renewal

Spark plugs are fitted to petrol engines (diesel engines don't have them), and their job is to ignite the air/fuel mixture in the cylinders at the correct moment.

Over time, the spark plugs deteriorate, and this can cause the engine to run inefficiently or to misfire, so it is important to change them at the recommended intervals, usually around every two years or 20,000 miles. Some special 'long-life' spark plugs may only need changing every 60,000 miles or five years, or even less frequently and are often fitted to engines where changing the plugs is a time-consuming operation.

On some cars, particularly older ones, changing the spark plugs is a simple operation, which will only take 10 minutes or so. On many modern cars though, access to the spark plugs is difficult, and a number of components need to be removed before you can reach them. Very often, although not always, it's time-consuming rather than difficult. If you decide you want to have a try, then consult the Haynes Manual for your car, which will contain step-by-step instructions.

TOOLS AND EQUIPMENT REQUIRED

* Spark-plug socket of the correct size, a ratchet and extension bar.
* New spark plugs of the correct type for your car.

Spark-plug gap

The gap between the spark plug electrodes is important, and it can cause problems with the running of the engine if the gap is incorrect. Most new spark plugs are supplied 'pre-gapped', but it's always as well to check that the gap is correct. The gap can be checked using a special plug-gap checking tool or 'feeler blades', and the figure for the recommended gap, and details of how to check, can be found in your car's handbook or Haynes Manual.

Here's a typical example showing how to change the spark plugs on a Ford Fiesta – this one is quite easy:

1 The four spark plugs are located at the top of the engine, and have thick 'HT' leads connected to them. It's a good idea to change one spark plug at a time, as it's vital that the correct lead is connected to the correct plug. If the leads are connected incorrectly, the engine will not run properly, and may not run at all!

2 Carefully pull the lead from the spark plug you want to change. Pull on the rubber connector at the end of the lead, not on the lead itself.

3 Using a spark-plug socket of the correct size, and a ratchet and extension bar, carefully unscrew the spark plug from the engine. The plug may be quite stiff to begin with.

4 With the old plug removed, push the new plug into the socket, so that it is held in place by the rubber grommet in the socket. It's important that the spark-plug gap is correct – see 'Spark-plug gap' panel.

5 Use your hand on the extension bar to carefully turn the socket until the spark plug begins to screw into the threads in the engine, then fit the ratchet to the extension bar and use it to screw the plug all the way in, taking great care not to over-tighten it.

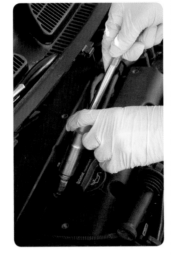

6 Push the lead connector firmly on to the end of the spark plug, making sure that it is securely connected. It should 'click' into place

7 Repeat the procedure for the remaining three spark plugs.

Timing belt ('cam belt') renewal

Most car engines have a timing belt, although some have a timing chain. Both the belt and chain perform the same function – they ensure that the engine's valves open and close at the correct time in relation to the movement of the pistons up and down the cylinders (see 'The engine' on pages 10–11).

If a timing belt is fitted, it must be renewed at the manufacturer's recommended intervals, as the belt is a critical engine component, and serious damage can result if the belt breaks when the engine is running. Timing chains don't normally need to be renewed.

Renewing a timing belt is a skilled job, particularly on modern, and often very complicated, engines, and it's definitely not a job for a novice! Special tools are often required, which may be specific to a particular engine type, and these can be very expensive and difficult to obtain. Depending on the car, a lot of dismantling may be required for access to the timing belt, and the time taken to complete the job can vary from around an hour, to as long as a working day for the most complicated examples.

A timing belt is made of rubber, which deteriorates with time and usage, therefore vehicle manufacturers recommend a specific mileage and time after which the timing belt must be renewed. These intervals vary greatly from one specific car to another, and may be as low as 40,000 miles/four years for some cars, and as high as 100,000 miles/ten years for others. It's vital that you get the timing belt changed at the recommended interval, because if it breaks, massive damage can be caused inside the engine. In the worst case, a repair bill for a broken timing belt can run into thousands of pounds, sometimes exceeding the value of the car. So ignore your car manufacturer's advice at your peril!

Garage servicing

Choosing a garage

If you need to have work done on your car, whether it's servicing, repair work, or fitting extras, how do you decide where to take it?

If your car is still under warranty, always ensure that the garage follow the manufacturer's schedule and use genuine parts.

If you want to ensure that your car has an authentic service history when you come to sell it, you may decide to have all work done by an authorised dealer. Generally, this will be the most expensive option, but you'll have the satisfaction of knowing that the manufacturer's procedures and parts will be used for all the work. When you come to sell, the car is likely to be worth more money and will be easier to sell.

If you're not prepared to pay the rates charged by an authorised dealer, you may decide to take your car to one of the smaller independent garages. Some specialise in a particular make of car and, although they may not be authorised dealers, you'll often find that their expertise is equal to, or even better than, that of the manufacturer's trained personnel. If you're going to take your car to an independent garage, it's always worth visiting several in your area, and asking them for a price for the work to be carried out.

At a smaller garage, you can't always expect the 'fancy' service provided by a larger dealer – there may not be a carpeted waiting area, and you may not be provided with a courtesy car, but remember that a dealer is building these 'perks' in to your bill.

Ask around to see if anyone you know has had a good or bad experience of dealing with any of the garages you're thinking of using. Reputation is very important, and it's often better to pay a little extra to take your car to a garage with a known good reputation.

Pricing

When asking for a price for work to be carried out, always ask for a written, firm price, and check to see what's included. Most authorised dealers have fixed-price 'menu' servicing costs, so you know exactly what you'll be paying for a particular service or job.

The items on a garage bill usually fall into one of three categories: parts, labour, and consumables. Parts include any new parts that may be required during the work. Labour covers the cost of the time taken (in hours) by the mechanic to carry out the work. Consumables covers items such as oil, coolant, cleaning fluids, etc. Always ask for an itemised list so that you can see exactly what's been included.

Here are a few things that you should ask when getting a price for a job:

* What's the hourly labour rate?
* How long should the work take?
* Will genuine or pattern parts be used?
* Is VAT included?
* Will the work be covered by a warranty? (Ask for details of the warranty.)

If you're comparing several quotes, make sure that you're making a fair comparison, as the prices may be structured differently. You should find that the prices are similar, and by comparing them you'll be able to spot any discrepancies or suspicious costs. If there's anything you don't understand, ask.

You can check the cost of genuine parts by asking at an authorised dealer, and you can compare these prices with those of pattern parts from a motor factor (pattern parts are aftermarket parts manufactured by third parties, rather than the manufacturer's genuine parts). There will always be a mark-up on parts prices, as a garage will almost certainly pay a 'trade' price for parts that will always be less than the retail price.

Once you decide to have the work done, ask the garage to contact you immediately if they encounter any problems that will involve additional work. If you don't do this, many will carry out the work anyway and charge you accordingly.

If you're having new parts fitted, check whether the work will be covered by a parts-and-labour warranty; if not, ask why.

Understanding the mechanic

When you're discussing any work to be carried out on your car, don't let the service manager or mechanic baffle you. Always ask if you have any questions. The Glossary at the end of this book should help you to understand the terminology used, and the explanations given in Chapter 1 should help too. Make sure that you understand what work the garage is intending to do.

Sometimes a garage may point out other potential problems whilst carrying out work on your car. For example, it might be suggested that the brake components are worn, and that you'll need new ones soon. Always check this for yourself, or ask the mechanic to show you the problem. If in doubt, ask for a second opinion from an experienced friend or another garage.

Checking the work

If components have been renewed, many garages leave the old components in a box in the boot, so that you can see that the work has been carried out, and to confirm that it was necessary. It's a good idea to ask the mechanic to do this when you take your car in for work to be done.

If your car has been serviced, check that a new (clean) oil filter has been fitted, and pull out the dipstick to check for fresh oil. Often, you can spot the areas where work has been carried out, because the areas surrounding the work will be cleaner than the rest of the car.

Checking the bill

Always ask for an itemised bill, which will give you a full breakdown of all the costs, and will allow you to see exactly what work has been carried out. Here are a couple of tips for checking that the bill is correct:

✱ Check the details of the bill against the firm price that you were given, and query any discrepancies. If you find that 'miscellaneous' costs appear on your bill, ask what they are.

✱ Check the labour costs against the garage's quoted hourly rate, and check that the price of any parts used seems reasonable.

Warranties

When you have work carried out on your car, the work should be covered by a warranty. If you have any work done that involves the fitting of new components (especially major items such as an engine or gearbox), make sure that the work and components are covered by a 'parts-and-labour' warranty. This will cover you against the use of any faulty parts, and any mistakes made by the mechanic that might cause trouble later. Check that the bill states the work is covered by a warranty, and be sure that the warranty period is specified.

THE MoT TEST

The annual MoT (Ministry of Transport) inspection is a cause for concern for many motorists. The test has changed quite a lot since it was first introduced in 1960, and currently applies to all vehicles over three years old – a car's first MoT is due on the third anniversary of its original registration date. Although the MoT testing scheme is now run by a government sub-department called VOSA (Vehicle and Operator Standards Agency), the origins of the name, Ministry of Transport, has stuck. Hence MoT.

Once your car is three years old, it's a legal requirement to have a valid MoT certificate, and unless you're driving to or from a test, driving a car on the road without a valid MoT is an offence and will invalidate your insurance. Make sure you keep a note of the MoT expiry date as, unlike car tax, you will not automatically be sent a reminder!

Over the years, the test has become much more substantial and complex, and now includes checks on components such as steering, suspension, lights, brakes, seatbelts, wheels and tyres, the driver's view of the road and, of course, the dreaded exhaust-emissions test. Currently, MoT tests are carried out 'live' online, and the tester has to enter the car's details on to a computer system as the test is carried out in order to be able to issue a certificate. This guards against forgery and fraud, and also helps to maintain testing standards.

Simple checks to avoid an MoT test failure

There are a number of things you can easily check yourself before taking your car for an MoT test, which can prevent unnecessary failure and possible expense. I will now explain these relatively simple checks, and the rules surrounding them, before moving on to items that you may not be able to check yourself, but that it may benefit you to know about. Note that this is not a complete list of checks, but provides a summary of those checks that can easily be carried out without specialist knowledge.

DON'T ASSUME THAT BECAUSE YOUR CAR HAS A FRESH MOT CERTIFICATE, IT HAS BEEN CERTIFIED AS SAFE!

Only items listed in the MoT Inspection Manual as 'testable items' have to be inspected, which means that some potentially dangerous faults will not prevent your car from being given a pass certificate, although if an inspector notices anything dangerous during the inspection, they will usually advise the car's owner. There is in fact an option available to the tester during the MoT procedure called 'advisories', which allows a tester to advise the owner of any issues that are not covered by the test, and to also tick a box if they are considered dangerous. A good example of this is worn brake components – the brakes may work fine, but the components may be so worn that they need to be replaced. And yes – the customer walks away with an MoT certificate for their car – crazy but true!

LIGHTS

Checking the condition and operation of the lights is an easy place to begin. If you have a friend who can help you with these checks, it will only take a couple of minutes to complete them. It's your responsibility to make sure that **all** your car's lights work every time you drive the car – if any are defective, you could be stopped by the police and possibly fined.

* Firstly, you need to check the operation of the front side-lights, rear tail-lights and all the hazard-warning lights with the engine and ignition switched off. This is to ensure that they work in case of an accident or breakdown.
* These lights also need to work with the ignition switched on, and note that some vehicles have a separate switch for side-lights when the ignition is on. The tail-lights should not show any white light to the rear, so if a lens is broken, and white light is visible, this will result in an MoT failure. All front lights, except the indicators, must provide white light.
* Next, check the indicators. On each side of the car there should be one at the front, a front side repeater (sometimes in the front wing or the mirror housing), and one at the rear. Check both the left and right indicators, and make sure that all three bulbs on the relevant side flash an amber colour, between 60 and 120 times per minute. Often, over time, the amber bulbs or lenses

deteriorate and flash white. Again this will result in a failure. Also check that the indicator warning lights on the dashboard flash to tell you that the indicators are operating.

✳ Also check that all the indicator lights flash when the hazard-warning-light switch is operated. Again, the hazard-warning light on the dashboard must flash when the hazard flashers are operated (this light is sometimes built into the switch).

✳ The headlights must work on both dipped and main beam, and the headlight pattern on dipped beam must be within certain specifications. While you will not be able to check the exact specification, pointing your car at a white wall or similar will allow you to assess whether the lights are even in height, and whether the dipped beam has what is known as a 'kick-up' (a 15-degree wedge of light from the centre which points towards the left). This 'kick-up' helps you to see the edge of the road when facing oncoming traffic in the dark.

✳ The rear number-plate light(s) must work when your side or headlights are on – this is another common failure point, and a light that often gets overlooked when performing weekly checks.

✳ Next, check your brake lights. Again, these should not show any colour other than red. If you have a high-level brake light, this does not need to work for the MoT, but if it's an LED strip, and some but not all of the bulbs work, it will fail! This check is easiest to carry out with the help of a friend, or with the car backed up against a wall or garage door so that you can see the brake lights illuminate when the pedal is pressed.

✳ Finally, check the rear fog light. Again, it should be red, and must be positioned on the right side of the car, although some cars have rear fog lights on both sides. A rear fog light warning light must also illuminate on the dash.

✳ Finally, turn on all the lights, and ensure that they do not affect each other's operation. Common problems include one light dimming, or not working when others are switched on, or brake or tail-lights flashing when the indicators are switched on. These problems are normally caused by a wiring fault, corrosion, or an incorrectly fitted bulb. Details of how to try and fix this can be found in the 'Fixing a faulty light' sidebar on page 47.

DRIVER'S VIEW

During the MoT, the driver's view of the road is checked, and this involves a number of separate checks that can easily be carried out at home. The checks involve the windscreen, and also washers, wipers and mirrors.

✳ Check the windscreen for chips and cracks. During the MoT, the screen will be checked in two different areas known as Zone A and Zone B. Both zones are located in the area your windscreen wipers clean. Any damage outside this 'swept area' will not cause a fail, but may result in an 'advisory'. Zone A is the area in the driver's direct forward field of vision, and any damage (chips or cracks) larger than 10mm (a 10mm circle around the centre of the damage) in this area will fail. Zone B is the rest of the windscreen area that the wipers cover, and in this area any damage must be smaller than 40mm in diameter to obtain a pass.

✳ Items such as furry dice or an air freshener hanging from the interior mirror, or a sat-nav stuck to the windscreen, are considered to affect the driver's view, so are best removed before the MoT.

✳ Official stickers on the windscreen that are not readily removable, such as tax discs, parking and access permits will only cause a problem if they seriously restrict the driver's view. However, a banner saying 'Gavin and Stacy' or similar is a definite no-no!

✳ Check that the windscreen washers work, and that they provide

enough washer fluid to allow the wipers to effectively clear the screen. The wiper blades must not produce smears or streaks, and the rubbers must not be split.

✳ A driver's side sun visor which cannot be fixed in the 'off screen' ('up') position, and which drops down, obstructing the view through the swept area of the windscreen, will result in a failure. A similar problem on the passenger side sun visor is not a problem.

✳ Finally, check the rear-view mirrors. At least two mirrors must be fitted, and only the driver's side wing mirror is compulsory. Mirrors should provide a clear view to the rear, and must be secure. Grasp each mirror and 'wiggle' it to check security.

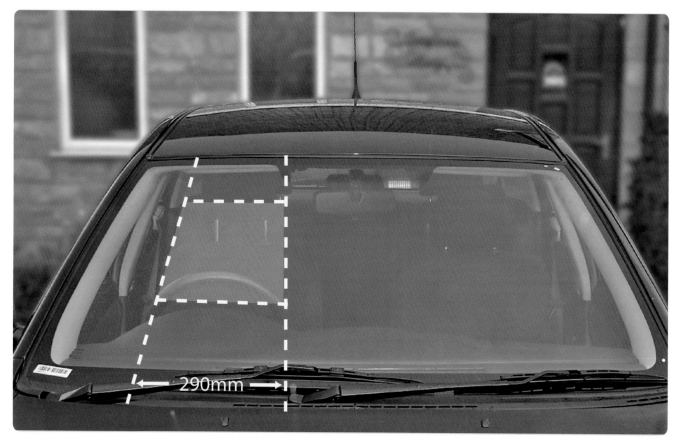

290mm

Checks made from inside the car

There are a few more checks that you can do from inside the car that could avoid an MoT failure.

* **Seats** – Check the security of all the seats, by grasping the base and the back of each seat and making sure that they are securely fixed. Additionally, it must be possible to move the driver's seat forwards and backwards, and lock it in all its different positions.

* **Seatbelts** – Check the condition and operation of the seatbelts. Pull each seatbelt out fully and check for cuts and fraying. Check that the seatbelt fixing points to the car are secure. Plug the end of the belt into its buckle, and ensure it fastens securely and will release under tension – pull on the seatbelt with one hand, and press the release button with the other. This check is made for safety reasons, to make sure belts will come undone in an accident, where there is tension on the seatbelt – for example if the car is upside down.

* **Doors and boot lid/tailgate** – The front driver's and passenger's doors should open from both the inside and outside of the car, and the rear doors (where fitted) must open from the outside. All the doors must also latch securely shut (for obvious reasons). The door hinges and catches are also checked to make sure that they are present, secure and that they work properly. The boot or tailgate does not need to open, but must be securely latched.

* **Horn** – Next, check that the horn works, is loud enough to be heard by other road users, and emits a continuous single tone. (Horns that play tunes are not permitted!)

* **Speedometer** – Check that the speedometer works – hopefully you will have noticed this when driving!

* **Brake pedal** – With the engine switched off, pump the brake pedal a few times and then, keeping pressure on the pedal, start the engine. The pedal should travel downwards as the engine starts, indicating that the brake servo (a device that helps apply the brakes) is working correctly. With the engine still running, make sure that the pedal doesn't feel really spongy, as this could indicate air in the hydraulic system, and make sure that you can't press the pedal all the way to the floor. Also check that the brake pedal rubber pad isn't excessively worn.

* **Handbrake** – The efficiency of the handbrake will be checked, so you might want to park the car on a hill and test it (keep your foot over the brake pedal in case you need to apply it!). If your car won't hold still on a hill, the handbrake mechanism will need adjustment or repair.

* **Warning lights** – Start your engine and ensure that, where fitted, the following warning lights on your dashboard illuminate and then go out after a few seconds. If any stay illuminated, this indicates a fault, and will result in a failure.

  o Electronic power steering warning light (sometimes labelled 'EPS').
  o Brake fluid level warning light.
  o Seatbelt pre-tensioner, air bag or 'SRS' warning light.
  o Handbrake warning light.
  o Tyre pressure monitoring light.
  o ABS warning light.

Checks made from outside the car

There are a few more checks that you can carry out from outside the car, which could just prevent an MoT failure.

* **Bodywork** – Check the bodywork for any sharp edges that are likely to cause injury – for example damage or rust, such as rusty wheel arches, or even a plastic bumper that's cracked. Although it's best to repair or replace these items, covering them with tape so the sharp edges are no longer protruding will prevent an MoT failure.

* **Tyres and wheels** – Tyres and road wheels will be checked for condition, and are a very common cause of MoT failure. Tyres worn below the legal limit are dangerous and illegal, and can result in penalty points and a hefty fine. The tyre's tread depth must be a minimum of 1.6mm over the centre three-quarters of the tyre's width. There must be no bulges in the tyre. Other reasons for failure include any cut more than 25mm in length that exposes the tyre cords (metal braids), or a damaged wheel rim. Both front tyres must be of the same size, as must both rear tyres, although on some cars the sizes may possibly be different

from front to rear. More details about checking tyres can be found in Chapter 3, on pages 40–42.

* **Brakes** – When you're driving the car, listen to check if the brakes make any noise when you apply them, and check that the car stops in a straight line. A scraping or grinding noise often indicates that the brakes are severely worn, and if the car pulls to one side when braking, this may be due to an imbalance in the braking system. Both of these problems will result in an MoT failure.

* **Exhaust** – The condition and security of the exhaust system will be checked and, if there's a serious 'blow' (a hole that's allowing exhaust gas to escape), which you may be able to hear (in severe cases your car may sound like a tractor!), the car will definitely fail! If you think your exhaust may be loose, which can cause unusual knocking or squeaking noises when driving, it may be due to worn or broken exhaust mountings, which can also be a reason for MoT failure.

* **Fuel filler cap** – Remove the fuel filler cap, and check that the rubber sealing ring that seals it to the fuel filler neck is in one piece and in good condition. Sometimes you may hear a 'whooshing' noise when you remove the cap, which indicates that the rubber seal is working. Some 'emergency' filler caps that you can buy as a temporary measure at filling stations will cause an MoT failure, as they don't form a good enough seal.

Checking for corrosion

There are a number of areas on your car, called 'prescribed areas', that will be checked for corrosion. They relate to the safety of steering, suspension, braking and seatbelt mounting points, as well as the general vehicle structure. Many of these 'prescribed areas' are underneath the car, so you may not be able to assess those yourself. However, one very common failure on ageing cars is corrosion to the sills. The sills are an important part of the vehicle structure, and run along each side of the car, underneath the doors.

The sills are easy to check, but quite low to the ground, so find a mat or some cardboard to kneel or lie on. Note that on some sporty models, or cars fitted with styling kits, the sills may be covered by plastic trim panels, and you may not easily be able to check them. Inspect the sill on each side of the car for holes or rusty areas. If there's obvious rust, use finger and thumb pressure to see if the rusty area is weakened. The metal should not flex when pushed.

If your car's sills, or any other areas, need to be repaired, this will need to be carried out by somebody who is experienced in welding repairs for

MoT requirements. Sometimes it may be possible to weld in a repair patch, but it may be necessary to fit a replacement sill or floor panel. To find a competent welder, ask for recommendations from friends, family or your local MoT station.

Wheel bearing

This sits inside the hub, to which the wheel is bolted, and allows the wheel to rotate smoothly and freely. Wheel bearings wear over time, causing 'play' (wobble) in the wheel and/or roughness when it rotates. A worn wheel bearing often causes a droning noise, which increases with the car's speed and sounds very similar to an aircraft preparing for take-off! If you think your car may have a worn wheel bearing, get it checked and if necessary renewed.

Number plate

The number plates will be checked during the MoT. An easy job you may think? With 16 reasons for rejection, perhaps not, and hard work to remember when you're testing!

Straight from the MoT Tester's Manual, here are the possible reasons for failure:

1 Missing or incorrect registration plate.
2 So insecure that it's likely to fall off.
3 Letter or figure missing, or incomplete.
4 Faded, dirty, delaminated, deteriorated or obscured, (for example by a towbar) so that it's likely to be misread, or is not easily legible by a person standing approximately 20 metres to the front/rear of the vehicle.
5 Background overprinted or shadowed with text – eg, vehicle manufacturer's name.
6 A front plate that does not have black characters on a white background.
7 A rear plate that does not have black characters on a yellow background.
8 A plate not fixed vertically, or as close to vertical as is reasonably practical.
9 Characters obviously not the correct height, character width, stroke width, not of equal width along their entire length or incorrectly spaced (distance 'A' must be at least twice distance 'B' in the illustration below).
10 A character not correctly formed, sloping, or likely to be misread.
11 Any feature that has the effect of changing the appearance or legibility of any of the characters, so that the true identity of the vehicle is less easily established.
12 Characters formed using a font which is not substantially similar to the prescribed font.
13 Characters formed using broken or multiple strokes.
14 Characters laid out in an incorrect format.
15 A margin obviously less than the minimum requirement.
16 A non-reflective border obviously wider than permitted, or positioned too close to the characters.

There are however exemptions for classic car plates, which can display silver characters on a black background.

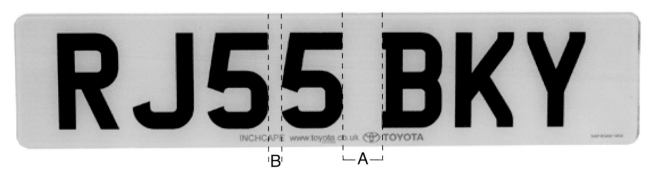

Checks under the bonnet

Contrary to what many people believe, no checks are carried out on the engine during an MoT test (with the exception of testing the exhaust emissions). However, a number of items under the bonnet are checked. Here are a few simple checks that you can carry out. See Chapter 3 for more details on how to carry out these checks.

* **Bonnet catches** – Check that the main bonnet catch and the secondary 'safety' catch (which prevents the bonnet opening if the main catch fails) are secure, and work correctly.
* **Brake fluid level** – Check that the brake fluid level is above the 'minimum', or 'MIN' level mark on the reservoir.
* **Coolant level** – Check that the coolant level is above the 'minimum', or 'MIN' level mark on the reservoir.
* **Battery** – Check that the battery is secure, and does not have any obvious leaks.

Checks carried out by the MoT tester

If we listed every further check covered by the MoT, this chapter would become a book in itself! To find out exactly what else is checked during the MoT test, you can download a copy of the full Inspection Manual from the VOSA website, but be warned, its 205 pages are not for the faint-hearted! You can also find more comprehensive details of the MoT test in the Haynes Manual for your car.

Refusal to test

When you take your car to have an MoT, the tester can refuse to test it for a number of reasons. Here are some reasons that can easily be avoided with a little preparation.

* The vehicle, or any part or equipment on the vehicle, is so dirty that examination is unreasonably difficult.
* The vehicle is not fit to be driven, due to lack of fuel, oil or any other reason.
* The tester considers the insecurity of a load, or other item, would prevent a proper test being carried out.
* The testing station asks for the fee to be paid in advance and this is not done.
* A proper examination cannot be carried out because a device such as a door, bonnet, fuel cap, etc, which is designed to be opened, cannot be.

Finding a good MoT testing station

There are currently around 22,000 MoT testing stations in the UK, so there are plenty to choose from! It's worthwhile taking some time to find a good one though, as although most garages offering MoT tests are reputable and friendly, unfortunately there are also some rogue, unscrupulous ones.

Often, the best way to find a good garage, as with many things, is to ask friends, family or colleagues for recommendations. You might also like to visit a few garages in the local area to get a 'feel' for how they treat their customers.

Don't always go for the cheapest garage. At the time of writing, the MoT recommended fee stands at £54.85, but testing stations don't have to charge this. They can discount the price as much as they wish, or even offer a free test, although they must not charge more than the recommended fee.

An unscrupulous garage might test your car for a £20 fee, but they might then fail the car on things that they shouldn't, resulting in a much larger bill than was necessary.

Finally, bear in mind that you have a right to watch your car being tested, and a testing station must provide a specific room or area for you to do so. Wherever possible, it's a good idea to take the opportunity to do this, as the tester is not to know that you are not an expert, or even one of the 'mystery shoppers' that VOSA sometimes send out in an effort to ensure that standards are maintained. Hopefully, you'll keep them on their toes!

If you're unable to watch the MoT, ask the garage to call you if your car fails, before carrying out any remedial work. That way, you can ask for a quote for the work, and you'll know what to expect. Also ask the garage to show you any original worn or damaged parts removed, so that you can be sure that the work did need to be done. It's a good idea to take a knowledgeable friend, relation or colleague with you if you're uncertain about any aspects of the test or the work carried out.

PROBLEMS

The following pages contain some useful information on common problems with cars, how to avoid them, and what to do if you're unfortunate enough to find yourself in any of the situations mentioned.

Common breakdowns and how to avoid them

Here are ten of the most common causes of breakdowns, with advice on how to avoid them, and suggestions on what to do if you're unlucky enough to be a victim of one of these problems.

1 Flat or faulty battery

If your car's battery is flat, when you go to start your car it will turn over slowly or not at all. Flat batteries can be caused by leaving electrical circuits switched on, such as the headlights, car stereo, or courtesy light, or could simply be due to the battery being old and in need of renewal. Often, a weak battery will fail on the first cold day of winter, as the cold affects a battery's performance. Many garages offer a free pre-winter check, which is well worth considering, to reduce the chances of getting stranded at the first sign of frost! Here are some other preventative measures you can take:

* Check the battery terminals regularly, make sure that they're secure and keep them free from corrosion. Most car accessory shops sell battery-terminal protector spray, or you can use petroleum jelly or grease instead.
* If you make lots of short journeys, take your car on a long journey every once in a while, which will help to charge the battery.
* Make sure that all the electrical equipment (lights, heater blower, heated rear window, etc) is turned off before you try to start the engine.
* At the first sign of trouble – such as difficult starting, dim headlights when the engine is idling, or if the red charging warning light on the dashboard comes on – have the battery tested.

2 Flat or damaged tyre, or damaged wheel

Getting a puncture, or damaging a wheel or tyre by hitting a pothole or kerb is often unavoidable, but here are some measures you can take to help prevent or minimise the damage:

* Check the tyre pressures and the condition of the tyres regularly. Don't forget the spare.
* Make sure that if you're carrying a heavy load you adjust the tyre pressures to the recommended 'full-load' pressures, and that you return them to normal when you've unloaded.
* If you 'kerb' a wheel when parking or driving, or encounter a nasty pothole, then check the condition of the wheel and tyre as soon as possible afterwards.
* Consider carrying a can of tyre 'instant repair' foam. This won't help if there's a massive hole in the tyre, but for small leaks it can be an effective, temporary solution.
* Make sure that the jack, wheel brace and (where applicable) the key or removal tool for locking wheel bolts, are in the car. If you've practised the steps in 'Changing a wheel', on pages 90–93, then you should be able to change the wheel yourself if necessary or, failing that, a breakdown company or a kind passer-by may be able to help you.

3 Alternator faults

The alternator is driven by a belt on the engine, and its job is to charge the battery. If the alternator fails, the battery will soon fail too, and if you're driving, the car may simply cut out and fail to restart – quite a scary experience, particularly in the fast lane of a motorway! The tell-tale signs of a problem include:

* Frequent battery problems and dim headlights when the engine is ticking over.
* A squealing sound from the engine compartment, which may indicate a slipping alternator drive belt.
* A glowing red charging warning light and/or an illuminated battery light on the dashboard, especially when the engine is ticking over.
* Stop as soon as possible if the charging warning light comes on when you're driving, and call your breakdown cover provider if you have one. Alternatively, stop at the nearest garage or petrol station to ask for advice.

4 Starter motor failure

The starter motor spins your car's engine over fast enough to start it, which can take its toll over time, particularly if you use your car for a lot of journeys that involve stopping and restarting the engine. The following signs are likely to indicate that the starter motor has failed:

* Metallic noises when trying to start the engine.
* The engine turns more slowly than usual when you try to start it (might also indicate a battery problem).
* When the ignition key is turned to the 'start' position, a click can be heard from the engine compartment, but the engine doesn't turn over (might also indicate a battery problem).
* The only cure is to get the starter motor replaced.

5 Misfire problems

An engine that is misfiring will usually suffer a loss of power, particularly when going uphill. It may also judder or shake, and you might notice that it doesn't sound normal. You might also have difficulty getting the car to start, particularly in cold or damp weather. There are a number of things that can cause a car to misfire – most of them are related to the car's electrics or fuel system. Here are the most common causes of misfire problems:

* Faulty ignition system component(s) – petrol-engined car. The ignition system provides the spark at the spark plug to ignite the fuel in the engine.
* A faulty spark plug – petrol-engined cars.
* Faulty fuel system component(s).
* A blocked fuel filter. The fuel filter removes dirt and debris to stop it getting into the engine, and over time the filter can become clogged with dirt and restrict the flow of fuel. This problem is more common on diesel engines.
* The wrong type of fuel, or the car running out of fuel – see page 80.
* A blown head gasket – see page 81.
* While it's often possible to drive a car with a misfire by 'nursing' it home, or to a garage, it's a good idea to call for breakdown assistance if you have cover, just in case driving further causes more damage to the engine.

6 Running out of fuel, or filling with the wrong type of fuel

WHAT TO DO IF YOU RUN OUT OF FUEL

* Don't keep on trying to start the engine, hoping to pick up the last drops of fuel from the tank – you'll suck air, and possibly dirt from the empty tank, into the fuel system, which will make starting even harder when you've filled up.
* If you have a can of fuel, switch off the ignition and empty the fuel into the fuel filler. Operate the starter for short – say ten-second – bursts, and if the engine now starts, drive on and fill the tank at the next filling station. If the engine still won't start, dirt or air drawn into the fuel system could be causing problems, in which case you'll probably need professional help.
* If you're out in the middle of nowhere, or on a motorway, all's not lost – if you're a member of one of the motoring organisations, they'll deliver an emergency can of fuel to you.
* If the fuel gauge indicated plenty of fuel in the tank, and you still ran out, have the gauge checked. If there's a fuel leak, you should be able to smell the petrol vapour or diesel – don't drive the car until you've had the problem fixed.
* On diesel-engined cars, if you've run out of fuel, the engine may be difficult to start even when you've refilled the tank. This is due to air being drawn into the fuel lines. Most diesel

cars are fitted with a hand priming pump (refer to your car's handbook or Haynes Manual) in the fuel system to get the engine started. Normally, the pump takes the form of a large pushbutton on top of the fuel filter, or a rubber bulb in one of the fuel lines. Switch on the ignition, then pump the priming button or bulb until you feel resistance (this could take more than 30 presses), indicating that the air has been expelled. Try to start the engine with the accelerator fully depressed – it should eventually start. If it still won't start, air has probably been drawn into the fuel-injection pump, in which case you'll need to seek professional help.

WHAT TO DO IF YOU FILL UP WITH THE WRONG FUEL

✳ If you've filled the tank with the wrong fuel, don't try to start the engine – if you do, it won't run for long, and you'll need to have all the fuel system components thoroughly cleaned and checked, which could be expensive! On some engines you can also cause very expensive damage.

✳ You'll need to have the fuel tank drained, cleaned and refilled with the correct fuel before you can drive the car – call for help. Note that if you have breakdown cover, this may not be included in your policy unless you've added it as an extra, so although the breakdown company will probably be happy to come out to you and fix the problem, they'll charge you a fee for doing so. Alternatively, as this is such a common problem, the filling station may be able to give you the telephone number of a company who can help.

Both of these problems are easily avoidable, provided you take the following precautions:

✳ Fill up with fuel before a long journey.

✳ Keep an eye on your fuel gauge, and don't wait until the warning light comes on before filling up. Fuel gauges can be notoriously inaccurate!

✳ If you're travelling on a road where fuel stations are scarce, make sure you have enough fuel to make it to the next large town where there's likely to be fuel available.

✳ If you're driving a new car, or you've hired or borrowed a car, make sure you know what type of fuel it takes, and always make sure that you've selected the correct fuel pump (petrol or diesel) before starting to fill up.

✳ Put an obvious sticker inside the fuel flap stating which fuel the car uses. These can be bought from motoring centres and some fuel stations.

7 Clutch failure

Sometimes clutches fail suddenly and without warning. In this case the car will need to be recovered, however, in many instances the symptoms occur gradually. If you experience any of the symptoms below, get the car checked as soon as possible to prevent a breakdown.

Common symptoms include:

✳ The car appears to 'rev' under acceleration, particularly in higher gears.

✳ The clutch feels 'strange' when you press the clutch pedal, or the pedal seems to be higher or lower than normal when in its rest position.

✳ The clutch pedal offers no resistance.

✳ The gears crunch when changing gear.

✳ Gears are hard or even impossible to engage.

8 A broken suspension spring

With the ever-increasing number of speed bumps, many of which are huge, the suspension on your car can take a daily battering. Add to this poor road surfaces, potholes etc, and it's no wonder suspension-component failures are on the increase. The most common and potentially problematic and dangerous of these is a broken coil spring. A corroded spring can snap at any time and without warning. If it breaks close to the end you may not notice, and it could go undetected until your next MoT or service. However, it's possible that a breakage could cause a sudden drop in the suspension at one corner and could also puncture the tyre. So, if you receive an advisory about a spring at an MoT or service, don't ignore it, as there's no way of knowing when a spring might break.

9 Engine overheating

Overheating is a serious problem, and can be caused by a number of things. If you're driving on a hot day in summer, your car will overheat much more easily in traffic than on a cold winter's day, but provided it's been properly maintained you shouldn't really have any problems.

When the engine gets hot, the cooling fan should cut in to lower the temperature. Normally you'll be able to see this on the temperature gauge – the temperature will go up until the cooling fan cuts in, then the temperature will fall. The cycle might repeat several times until you start moving forwards fast enough for the airflow to cool the radiator without needing the fan.

If the temperature gauge (or warning light) stays in the red, don't be tempted to carry on driving – stop as soon as possible.

Here are the most common causes of overheating:

* Low coolant level.
* Faulty cooling fan.
* Coolant leakage.
* Faulty coolant pump.
* Faulty thermostat.
* Blown head gasket.

WHAT TO DO IF YOUR ENGINE OVERHEATS

Cars most often overheat when stuck in traffic, so keep an eye on the temperature gauge.

* If you notice the temperature gauge needle creeping towards the red, or if a temperature warning light comes on, try moving the heater control to 'hot' straight away, and switch the heater blower motor to maximum – this will get rid of some of the heat from the engine. If the temperature doesn't drop, or keeps going up, pull over in a safe place and stop the engine.
* If you notice steam coming from under the bonnet, pull over and stop as soon as possible. Don't open the bonnet until the steam stops.
* If no steam is coming from under the bonnet, open the bonnet to help the heat escape, and wait for the engine to cool down. A very hot engine takes time to cool, and you'll have to wait at least half an hour before the temperature drops to normal.
* Check under the car for coolant leakage – coolant is usually brightly coloured (often green, yellow or pink), and will probably be steaming if it's hot. If there's a leak, call for assistance.
* When the engine has cooled, if there's no obvious sign of leakage, check the coolant level – if there's been no leakage, and no steam, the level will probably be above the 'maximum' mark (hot coolant expands). If the coolant level is OK, and there's no leakage, it's safe to carry on driving, but keep an eye on the temperature gauge! If the coolant level is low, it's time to top up. You can use plain water in an emergency. If almost all the coolant has been lost, don't fill the cooling system with cold water whilst the engine is hot, as this might cause engine damage.
* Get the car checked by a garage as soon as possible.

10 Leaking cylinder head gasket

A leaking cylinder head gasket can be a big problem, and major work on the engine may be required to fix it. There's little that can be done to avoid this problem, but a major cause is engine overheating, so keep an eye on the temperature gauge from time to time, and if the temperature creeps towards the red zone, stop immediately and check the coolant level. The tell-tale signs of a problem include:

* A lack of power.
* Misfiring, especially when the engine is cold or when starting.
* Fluid leaks on the outside of the engine.
* Oil in the coolant – usually shows itself as a frothy 'mayonnaise'.
* Coolant in the oil – usually shows itself as a frothy 'mayonnaise'.
* A mysterious drop in coolant level, and the need for frequent topping up.
* Engine overheating.
* White smoke from the exhaust.

Warning and 'tell-tale' lights and what they mean

All cars are fitted with various warning lights to alert the driver to possible faults. Some warnings are more serious than others, so here's a guide to what the more common warning lights mean, and what to do if they come on. All the warning and tell-tale lights are usually explained in the car's handbook. **Note:** *Not all the warning lights described in the following paragraphs are fitted to all cars.*

Brake fluid level warning – This indicates low brake fluid level. Don't drive the car. Check the brake fluid level and top up if necessary. If the fluid level is low, have the car checked for brake fluid leaks, and don't drive it until the problem has been fixed. If the fluid level isn't low, it could indicate a faulty sensor, in which case after checking that the brakes work, the car can be driven carefully to a garage for checking.

Brake pad wear warning – This indicates that the brake pads are worn. The car can be driven. Have the pads checked and, if necessary, renewed as soon as possible, as worn brakes are not as efficient as new ones, and if the brake pads get really worn, they can damage the brake discs, causing considerably more expense. **Note:** *Occasionally the light can come on due to a faulty sensor, but a garage will be able to advise on this.*

Handbrake 'on' warning – This warns you that the handbrake is applied. The light can come on due to a poorly adjusted handbrake lever or a faulty switch. This light sometimes doubles as a low brake-fluid warning light – check your car's handbook for details.

Charge warning – This light warns that the alternator is not charging the battery, or that the battery is faulty. The car can be driven, but not far, as the battery may eventually go flat, causing the engine to stop. If you have

breakdown cover, call them out to check the car over, and if not, try to stop at the next garage if it's open. The garage or recovery person will check the alternator and its wiring, and will test the battery to see if there's a fault.

Oil pressure warning – This warning light indicates that the engine oil pressure is potentially damagingly low. Many people often incorrectly assume that this is an oil level warning light. While one cause of low pressure can be a dangerously low oil level, often by the time this light illuminates, serious damage has already been done to the engine. If the light comes on when driving, stop the engine immediately, check the oil level and look for leaks, then call for assistance. Serious and expensive damage could be caused if you carry on running the engine. If the light comes on when the engine is ticking over, but goes out when you 'blip' the throttle, the engine may be very hot or seriously worn. Again, check the oil level, top up if necessary and ideally avoid driving until the cause of the problem has been found.

Coolant temperature – This orange or red warning light shows that the coolant temperature has reached a dangerously high level. Some cars also have a blue light to indicate when the engine is below normal operating temperature. If the red or orange light comes on, stop as soon as possible, allow the engine to cool, then check the coolant level. Top up if necessary. If the light comes on again within a short distance, stop and call for assistance. See page 80 for more details.

Coolant level warning – Not fitted to all cars, this light comes on when a sensor detects that the coolant level is low. Stop as soon as possible and check the level. If the coolant needs topping up, and the engine is warm or hot, leave the engine to cool for at least 10 minutes before attempting to remove the filler cap, and then place a wad of cloth over the cap before removing it, to protect your hands from escaping steam. Top up the level using plain water. If the light comes on again, check for leaks and call for assistance.

Engine system warning (or MIL – Malfunction Indicator Light) – This light indicates that a fault is present in the engine's electronic management system, which has been detected by the car's self-diagnostic system. The car can be driven, but will need to be checked as soon as possible at a garage with computer diagnostic equipment to determine the cause of the light illuminating. Don't ignore the light, as you may cause more damage by continuing to drive the car. In certain instances this light may also cause the car's engine systems to go into 'safe' or 'limp-home' mode. This usually restricts the engine revs, leaves you with very little acceleration, and can also seriously restrict the top speed of the car (to as little as around 40mph), making it frustrating and potentially dangerous to drive. Get to a garage as soon as possible, or if you're a long way from home, consider recovery.

ABS warning – This light indicates that there's a problem with the anti-lock braking system (ABS). The normal braking system will not be affected, so the car can be driven, but you'll need to get the car checked by a garage with the appropriate diagnostic equipment as soon as you can. If this light is illuminated, it will also result in an MoT failure.

Air bag (or SRS – Supplementary Restraint System) warning – This light indicates that there's a fault either with an air bag, a sensor or another part of the SRS system, such as a seatbelt pre-tensioner. The car can be driven with the light on, but it should be checked urgently, as a fault in the system may mean that the potentially lifesaving air bags or other SRS systems will not activate in an accident. If this light is illuminated, it will also result in an MoT failure.

Electric power steering (EPS) warning – This light indicates that there's a problem with the power steering. If your power steering stops working, the steering wheel can become very heavy to turn and can

make the car potentially dangerous to drive, and very difficult to park. If the light comes on, it's best to stop driving and call your breakdown company or consult a garage.

Glow plug warning (diesel cars only) – This light illuminates when you switch on the ignition. It indicates that the glow plugs (heater plugs) are preheating the engine to aid starting. You should not turn the ignition key to the 'start' position until this light goes out. If it stays on when the car is running, it may indicate a fault with the glow plug system. This will need to be checked as soon as possible, as glow plug failure can prevent the car from starting, particularly in cold weather. This light sometimes also doubles as an engine fault warning light.

Low fuel warning – This light indicates that the fuel level is low, and you should refuel as soon as possible. Ideally, don't allow the level to get low enough for this light to come on.

Rear fog light indicator – This orange light tells you that the rear fog light is on. The rear fog light should be turned on when the visibility is less than 100 metres. If the visibility improves, don't forget to turn the fog light off, as to drive with it switched on in fine conditions is an offence.

Lights indicator – Fitted to many cars, this light (usually green) indicates that the car's lights are switched on.

Main beam indicator – This blue light indicates that you're driving with your headlights switched to main beam.

Heated rear screen indicator – This light reminds you that the heated rear screen is switched on. A heated screen is very handy on damp or frosty mornings, but can be a strain on the battery!

Diesel particulate filter (DPF) warning – This light usually means that the DPF needs cleaning. The DPF reduces the level of smoke particles released into the atmosphere. Cleaning of the filter is best carried out by a garage, using the manufacturer's recommended cleaner.

Tyre pressure warning – This light is intended to warn you that the tyre pressures are incorrect, but very often the fault is with the sensor in the tyre!

Noises

There are many different noises your car can make if something goes wrong, and an even larger number of ways I've heard them described! So, whether it's a knock, bang, clonk, rattle, squeal, squeak, screech, scrape, chuff, puff, hiss, patter – or something else entirely, this guide will help you to identify the possible cause of the noise, and decide whether it's something to get checked as a matter of urgency, or an annoyance that you can live with for a while.

NOISES FROM UNDER THE BONNET

A squealing noise – Often more prominent when you first start the engine, and which can get louder when you rev the engine, is often caused by a loose or worn auxiliary drive belt ('fan belt'). This is not a huge problem, but it can be very annoying. It's a good idea to have the problem checked out to avoid any risk of the belt breaking.

A continuous hum or whine – This could indicate that the timing belt or auxiliary drive belt is too tight. The noise could also be caused by a worn water pump, alternator, power steering pump, or belt pulley. It's a good idea to have the noise checked out just in case it's caused by a problem that might result in further damage or even a breakdown.

A rattling, tapping or knocking sound from the engine – A tapping noise on start-up, which often goes away once the engine is warm, may indicate sticking hydraulic tappets. These open and close the valves in the engine, and are prone to getting gummed up if the oil hasn't been changed regularly. Not a major problem, and can possibly be cured by using a flushing fluid to clean the engine. Rattling or knocking sounds can indicate a number of mechanical problems inside the engine, and are best checked as soon as possible.

A hissing noise from under the bonnet – Usually indicates an air leak in one of the hoses under the bonnet. This may affect the way the engine runs, and its fuel economy, so it's best to get the noise checked out as soon as you can.

A 'chuffing' noise from the engine on diesel cars – This is often accompanied by a smell of diesel. This is likely to indicate that one or more of the sealing washers on the fuel injectors has failed. This is a common problem on certain engines, and needs immediate attention.

NOISES FROM THE SUSPENSION AND STEERING

A pattering sound, especially when you go over a bump – The most likely cause of this noise is wear in suspension joints or rubber bushes. Even a small amount of wear can cause annoying noises – not usually dangerous, but they are only likely to get worse, so you should have the suspension checked as soon as you can.

A clonking sound when you hit a bump – Again, the most likely cause is wear in suspension joints or bushes, or perhaps worn steering components. Wear can be accompanied by a feeling that the car is 'floating' about on the road. In the worst cases, these problems can affect the handling of your car and can be potentially dangerous. It's best to get the cause of such noises checked as soon as possible.

A screech, squeal or whine when you turn the steering wheel – This noise may get worse when the steering is turned on full lock. This indicates a problem with the hydraulic power steering. Very often this is caused by low power-steering fluid level – check the fluid level as described in Chapter 3, and top it up if it's low. Once the fluid has been topped up, turning the steering from lock to lock a few times should get rid of the noise. If fluid has been lost, this is almost certainly due to a leak, which will need investigation. A worn power steering pump or auxiliary drive belt ('fan belt') could also be the cause of the problem. Get the car checked at a garage as soon as you can.

A clicking noise when you turn a corner – The most likely cause is a worn drive shaft joint, although it's possible you have a stone caught somewhere. A worn drive shaft joint will only get worse and will need to be renewed.

A droning noise similar to an aircraft preparing for take-off – This noise is likely to get more noticeable with speed. This is a very common noise and is most likely to be caused by a worn wheel bearing. Don't ignore this one – it will get worse and can be dangerous.

NOISES FROM THE EXHAUST

A slight chuffing or blowing noise, especially when accelerating – This is likely to be due to a small leak in the exhaust system. This is not a major problem, and is not dangerous, but get it fixed before it turns into a more serious and costly problem. Often, small cracks or holes can be welded to repair them, which saves on the cost of a new exhaust. A leaking exhaust will cause an MoT failure.

A loud roaring noise, similar to a racing car! – There is likely to be a large hole in the exhaust, or even a damaged section that has become detached. Check under the car to make sure there is nothing obvious hanging down, and then get the problem looked at straight away.

Metallic rattling or thumping – This is likely to be due to a broken exhaust mounting which is allowing the exhaust to bang against the underneath of the car. If it's very loud, you may have a piece of the exhaust dragging on the ground. Check under the car to see if there's anything obvious, and then get the car checked.

NOISES FROM THE BRAKES

A metallic scraping sound when the brakes are applied – Likely to be due to excessively worn brake components, but could be something such as a stone lodged in the brakes. Get the problem checked as soon as possible.

A chattering or tapping sound – This could be due to a small stone lodged in the brakes, or it could indicate that the brake friction material is breaking up. Get a garage to carry out a check in case further damage occurs.

A light squeaking noise – This can indicate corrosion, especially if the car hasn't been used for a while. It may be that the brakes are clogged with brake dust and need cleaning. It can also be a characteristic of disc brakes, which can often be cured by dismantling and treating with a specialist anti-squeal compound. Ask your local garage to check the cause for you. Note that you may find the brakes squeak the next morning after washing your car – this noise will normally stop quite quickly, and is nothing to worry about, as it's due to rust forming on the wet brake discs overnight.

CLUTCH AND GEARBOX NOISES

Whining noise when the clutch pedal is depressed – If this noise stops when the clutch is released, the likely cause is a worn clutch release bearing. This shouldn't cause a problem in the short term, but get the problem fixed fairly quickly before it develops into something more serious.

Whine or howl when the car is running and in neutral, which goes away when you press the clutch – This noise is likely to be due to a worn transmission bearing. Get the problem checked as soon as possible, as if a bearing fails, it can cause serious damage to the gearbox.

Crunching sound when changing gear – This noise is likely to be due to a worn clutch or gearbox internal components. Have the problem checked by a gearbox specialist before it develops into something more serious.

Fluid leaks

There are a number of different fluids that can leak from your car, and often a leak may show up as a stain on the ground, or you may be forever topping-up one of the fluids. Here's a quick guide to how to identify possible leaks, and whether or not it's safe to drive the car if you find a leak.

PETROL

Petrol has a strong and distinctive smell, so a leak should be obvious. If you've just filled up with petrol on a hot day, and the car's standing in the sun, the petrol may expand, and liquid or vapour may leak out through the fuel tank breather. Petrol can also leak if you park a car with a full tank on a steep slope. Petrol will evaporate very quickly, so you're unlikely to find a stain under the car. If the leak isn't due to either of these causes, have it investigated straight away. Don't drive the car until the leak's been fixed, as a petrol leak is a potentially dangerous fire hazard.

DIESEL FUEL

Diesel fuel has a distinctive oily smell (like domestic heating oil), and is a clear, oily substance. As with petrol, a recently filled tank may leak a little due to expansion. Any other leak is cause for concern. Don't drive the car until the leak's been fixed.

ENGINE OIL

Engine oil is usually black, unless it's recently been changed. Clean oil is usually a transparent golden colour. Compare the leak with the oil on the end of the oil dipstick (see Chapter 3). The most common sources of leaks are the oil drain plug, the oil filter, and the sump gasket under the engine. You can drive with a minor oil leak, but keep an eye on the oil level, and get the car checked by a garage as soon as possible.

COOLANT

Coolant usually contains a bright-coloured dye, and has a strong, sickly sweet smell. Old coolant may be rusty or dirty brown, and there may be a white crystalline deposit around the leak. Leaks usually come from a hose, the radiator, or the heater inside the car (you'll smell coolant when you switch the heater on). You can drive with a minor leak, but if you lose too much coolant, the engine could overheat. Check the level regularly and get the car checked as soon as you can.

WATER

If a leak looks like clear water, and your car has air conditioning, it may not be a leak but condensation from the air conditioning system. A lot of condensation can be produced on a hot day, which may look like a major leak.

BRAKE/CLUTCH FLUID

Brake/clutch hydraulic fluid is a transparent, very pale golden colour, thin and almost watery. Old hydraulic fluid gradually darkens. Compare the leak with the contents of the brake or clutch fluid reservoir on your car (see Chapter 3). Brake fluid leaks usually come from the area around or under the brake fluid reservoir in the engine compartment, but may also appear around the wheels or the brake pipe connections under the car. Clutch fluid leaks usually come from hydraulic pipe connections, or from failed seals in the hydraulic components.

Don't drive the car if you think there might be a brake fluid

leak. It's OK to drive with a minor clutch fluid leak, but if you lose all the fluid the clutch won't work, so it's safest to get the vehicle recovered to a garage.

MANUAL GEARBOX OIL

The oil is usually a tan colour or reddish-pink, although old oil may darken. Gearbox oil often has a very sickly smell, especially when hot.

You can drive with a minor leak, but if the oil level gets too low it can cause serious damage to the gearbox. As you can't easily check the oil level, take the car to a garage as soon as possible to prevent potentially expensive gearbox damage.

AUTOMATIC TRANSMISSION FLUID

The fluid is usually a pink colour, although some manufacturers use green or clear fluid. Leaks usually come from the transmission casing, or from fluid lines running to the fluid cooler (this could be mounted on the transmission, or incorporated in the radiator at the front of the engine compartment). You can drive with a minor leak, but low fluid levels can cause the automatic transmission to slip, or in some cases fail altogether. Very low fluid can cause expensive damage, so it's advisable to get the leak fixed as soon as you can.

POWER STEERING FLUID

The fluid is usually pink or green. Compare the leak with the contents of the power steering fluid reservoir (see Chapter 3). Leaks usually come from fluid pipe connections, the power steering pump, or the steering mechanism. If the fluid level becomes very low, the steering pump will make a horrible groaning noise when you turn the steering wheel, particularly on full lock. In this instance, top the reservoir up to the maximum, operate the steering from lock to lock a few times, then recheck the reservoir, topping up again if necessary. This should cure the noise. You can drive with a minor leak, but keep an eye on the fluid level and get it checked as soon as possible.

WASHER FLUID

Washer fluid usually contains a coloured dye, and has a strong smell of detergent, alcohol or ammonia. The leak could be due to a leaking or split pipe connection, a leaky washer pump, or a hole in the washer fluid bottle. You can drive the car, but get the problem fixed, as it's an offence to drive with an empty washer fluid bottle, and in poor conditions it can be dangerous if you can't clean your screen.

Starting problems

It can be frustrating and distressing if you get in to your car and it won't start, particularly if you're not at home. Here are some of the most common causes, along with checks that you can carry out before you call for help.

IF THE ENGINE TURNS OVER AS NORMAL, BUT DOESN'T START:

Check the fuel gauge to make sure that there's fuel in the tank – If a fuel tank is nearly empty, even though the engine many have been running fine before you stopped it, it may still later refuse to start, particularly if you've parked on a hill (in which case the fuel may run away from the pick-up pipe inside the tank). If the fuel gauge is showing nearly empty, add some fuel to the tank, but be aware that you might need to try starting for some time before the fuel reaches the engine. Also, on some diesel engines, a hand-operated priming pump under the bonnet may need to be used to draw fuel into the fuel lines. If you can locate this pump, you may be able to try this yourself (refer to your car's handbook or Haynes Manual), otherwise you may need to call for help.

Does your car have an immobiliser? – On some cars fitted with an engine immobiliser, the car will appear completely 'dead' – on others, the engine will turn over but not start. Try locking and unlocking the car with the buttons on the key fob, or with the key itself, before trying to start again. If this doesn't work, take the car to a garage for checking.

Does your car have a petrol engine? – It could be flooded (which means that there's too much fuel in the engine), which will stop it from starting. This can sometimes happen if you've started the car from cold and then stopped it again almost immediately, or sometimes it can happen for no apparent reason at all! The engine may sound slightly different when you turn the key, sometimes turning over faster than usual. Most cars have a built-in cure for this – press the accelerator pedal fully to the floor and hold it there, then turn the key for 20 seconds or so. If the engine starts, don't stop it again before you've driven the car 2–3 miles to make sure that any excess fuel is burnt off.

Does your car have a diesel engine? – It's possible that the 'glow plugs' (also known as heater plugs) are not working properly. Most diesel engines have glow plugs to start the engine from cold, and there's normally a warning light on the dashboard, which should go out before you turn the ignition key to the 'start' position. This problem often shows up on a particularly cold day. It sometimes sounds as if the engine is trying to start, but doesn't quite manage it. If not all the glow plugs are faulty (each cylinder in the engine has

its own glow plug), sometimes you may be able to get the car to start by turning the ignition on and off a few times, for 4–5 seconds, before trying to start. If this fails, you'll need to seek assistance.

IF NOTHING AT ALL HAPPENS WHEN YOU TURN THE IGNITION KEY:

The most common cause is a flat battery – This could be because it's been drained by an electrical circuit, such as lights or stereo, being left on. The problem could also be due to a faulty alternator, or the battery could just have 'died'. Often, a weak battery will fail at the first frost of winter, as the colder it is, the harder the battery finds it to start the engine. If you have very dim or non-existent dashboard lights, or your headlights are dim or not working, then a flat battery is very likely. If you have jump leads and another vehicle that runs, then it may be possible to jump-start the car. However, before attempting this, read the 'Jump-starting a car' procedure (opposite) very carefully. Failing this, you'll need to seek help.

Another common cause is a failed starter motor – In this case you'll often be able to hear a clicking noise when the ignition key is turned to the 'start' position, rather than the normal sound of the engine turning over. You may be able to 'bump-start' the car, but only attempt this if you, or somebody who can help you, have experience of bump-starting. It can be dangerous, and can also damage the catalytic converter in the exhaust system (due to unburned fuel passing in to it) if you get it wrong.

Does your car have an immobiliser? – See the details given under the 'If the engine turns over as normal, but doesn't start:' heading.

Jump-starting a car

Warning: *If you have a flat battery, it may be possible to jump-start the car, but it's also possible to cause damage to the car's electrical components, particularly the ECU (Electronic Control Unit – the car's 'brain'), which could result in a huge repair bill. Consult your car's handbook to ensure that your car is suitable for jump-starting – not all are – and if in any doubt, call for professional assistance. Note also that certain cars have special terminals that **must** be used for jump-starting.*

TO JUMP-START A CAR:

1 Position the two cars so that you can connect the batteries together using the jump leads, but **don't** let the vehicles touch. Switch off the ignition and all electrical equipment on both cars, make sure that handbrakes are applied, and make sure that the gears are in neutral (manual gearbox), or 'P' on automatic transmission models.

2 Connect one end of the RED jump lead to the positive (+) terminal of the flat battery. Don't let the other end of the jump lead touch any vehicle metal.

3 Connect the other end of the RED lead to the positive (+) terminal of the fully charged battery.

4 Connect one end of the BLACK jump lead to the negative (–) terminal of the fully charged battery.

5 Connect the other end of the BLACK jump lead to a bare-metal bolt or metal bracket, well away from the battery, on the engine of the car to be started.

6 Make sure that the jump leads can't come into contact with any moving parts of either engine, then start the engine of the car with the fully charged battery and run it at a fast tick-over.

7 Start the engine of the car with the flat battery, and make sure that it's running properly.

8 Stop the engine of the car with the fully charged battery, then disconnect the jump leads. Disconnect the BLACK lead first – from the car with the flat battery, and then from the car with the fully charged battery; then disconnect the RED lead – from the car with the fully charged battery first, then from the car with the flat battery.

9 Keep the use of electrical equipment to a minimum, and remember that it will take some time for the alternator to charge the flat battery. Don't stop the engine too soon, and try not to stall it whilst driving.

Changing a wheel

As the following steps will explain, changing a wheel is very straightforward, and anyone can do it, you just need time, patience and a bit of determination. However, attempting a wheel change for the first time on a country lane in the dark when you've discovered your mobile battery is flat, is not an ideal scenario. So, it's a good idea to practise a few times on your driveway to find out where the tools and spare wheel are kept, and to familiarise yourself with the procedure. You could also practise with a friend, or ask a more-experienced driver to help out.

If you pick up a puncture when you're driving, you'll probably notice the car 'pulling' to one side through the steering and, depending on how flat the tyre is, the car's handling is likely to be affected – the car may feel as if it's sliding when you turn a corner, as if you're driving on an icy road. If the tyre is completely flat, you may also notice a noise coming from the offending wheel.

If you think your car may have a puncture, stop as soon as possible, but don't panic – heavy braking with a serious puncture could cause you to lose control. Try to park safely, away from traffic. If you're at the side of a busy road, and you can't move the car, it's safer to call for assistance rather than risk an accident. Stop the car, switch on the hazard-warning lights, and set up your warning triangle, if you have one, to alert other road users, particularly in the dark.

TO CHANGE A WHEEL, PROCEED AS FOLLOWS:

1 Check that the car is parked on level, firm ground, and make sure that the handbrake is applied. Select first gear (manual transmission) or 'P' (automatic transmission). This is an additional safety measure to stop the car moving if your handbrake fails.

2 Get out the spare wheel, car jack and wheel brace. Your car may also have locking wheel nuts, in which case you'll need to locate the special key. This is often kept in the boot with the tools, but can also be found hidden in a number of places including the glove box, door pockets, ashtray, centre console, under the seats and anywhere else you can (or maybe can't) think of. For safety reasons, you should chock the wheel diagonally opposite the one to be changed, using a couple of wooden blocks, or large stones.

3 Where applicable, pull off the wheel trim. These can be quite tough to remove, so grab with both hands and give a sharp tug. Failing that, use a screwdriver to prise the trim loose. Some alloy wheels have a centre cap which covers the wheel bolts/nuts – a special tool is often needed to remove this. The tool should be located with the other tools in the boot. Some manufacturers also put plastic or metal covers over the wheel bolts/nuts – again there may be a special tool for their removal in the boot, or you may need to prise them off with a screwdriver. Once you have access to the wheel bolts/nuts, use the wheel brace to loosen each one on the affected wheel – don't unscrew the bolts/nuts too far at this stage, just slacken them.

Stiff wheel bolts

Often, the most difficult part of changing a wheel can be slackening the wheel bolts/nuts. All wheel bolts/nuts should be tightened to a specific torque (tightness) using a torque wrench. However, there are some garages that unfortunately don't follow this practice; instead they over-tighten the bolts/nuts using an air-wrench. If the car hasn't received proper maintenance, and the wheels haven't been removed for some time, then the bolts/nuts can rust, again making them difficult to remove.

The wheel brace supplied with your car is often very short, making it difficult to apply enough pressure to slacken the bolts/nuts, even if they are not over-tight. For this reason, it's a good idea to carry an extending wheel wrench, as the extra length will make it much easier to slacken the bolts/nuts. Occasionally, when wheels haven't been removed for a long time, especially with alloy wheels, the inside faces of the wheels can corrode and stick after the bolts/nuts have been removed. In this case, make sure that the car is securely supported, then kick the bottom of the wheel with the sole of your foot, rotate the wheel 90 degrees, and do the same again. Keep repeating this process until the wheel becomes free. It's a good idea to leave one of the bolts in place (but loose) when you do this, to stop the wheel falling off.

4 Locate the jack in the jacking point provided under the car – consult the car's handbook or Haynes Manual if you're unsure where this is. Slide the spare wheel partway under the side of the car, near the wheel to be removed, but out of the way of the jack (this is a safety measure to stop the car falling on the floor if the jack should fail). Raise the jack until the wheel is a few centimetres off the ground.

5 Remove the wheel bolts/nuts, put them somewhere safe, and lift off the wheel. Drag the spare wheel out from under the side of the car, and slide the removed wheel under the car in its place.

6 Fit the spare wheel, then refit the bolts/nuts, and tighten them until they're holding the wheel firmly.

7 Remove the wheel from under the car, then lower the jack and remove it from under the car.

8 Tighten one wheel bolt/nut securely, using the wheel brace, then tighten the one diagonally opposite. Tighten the other two bolts/nuts in the same way, then refit the wheel trim and the bolt/nut covers, where applicable.

9 When you've finished, place the removed wheel and the tools back in their correct locations. Check the pressure in the 'new' tyre with your gauge or at the next available garage. It's important to get the flat tyre repaired or renewed as soon as possible, so that you have a spare if you're unlucky enough to get a second puncture. It's also a good idea to have the wheel bolts/nuts checked at the first opportunity to make sure that they're tightened securely – ideally to the specified torque-wrench setting.

'Space-saver' spare tyres and tyre repair kits

Some cars have a space-saver spare wheel and tyre, because there isn't enough room in the car for a normal full-size spare.

These tyres are narrower than normal tyres, and are often inflated to a different pressure. Usually, there are speed and mileage restrictions marked on the tyre, or printed in the car handbook – you are often limited to a maximum speed of 40mph (65kph) and a distance of 40 miles (65km). Make sure you take note of these restrictions.

If you fit a space-saver tyre, drive as few miles as possible, find the nearest tyre centre, and have the 'normal' flat tyre repaired and refitted as a matter of urgency.

Some cars no longer come with a spare wheel at all, and instead you will be provided with a can of tyre foam, and often an electric compressor. These are great for small punctures, but if you have a huge cut in your tyre or have had a blow-out, it will be completely useless! However, even if you do have a spare, carrying a can of tyre foam as well can be a useful back-up measure if the wheel proves impossible to remove. Read the instructions on the can carefully, as they will inform you how far you can travel and at what speed.

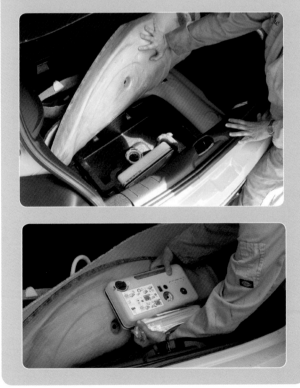

CLEANING

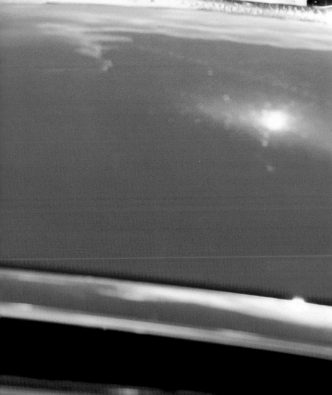

Keeping your car clean has several benefits. A clean and well-maintained car will be easier to sell than a scruffy one, and will have a higher market value.

With a few professional products, and a little bit of elbow grease, you can keep your car in showroom condition. Over the next few pages you'll find a guide to cleaning and maintaining the interior and exterior of your car, including stain removal, caring for paintwork, removing minor scratches and blemishes, and how to use touch-up paint. There are also a few money-saving trade secrets.

Exterior cleaning

Cleaning your car is something you can do cheaply and easily yourself with a bucket and sponge, or you may decide to use a car-wash or jet-wash, or you could take your car to one of the increasing number of 'hand car washes', where some nice people clean your car for you while you wait or go shopping!

Automated car-wash

This is a quick and easy option, but not to be recommended on a regular basis, as these machines often don't clean the car particularly well, and it's easy to spot a car that has frequently been put through a car-wash, as it will often have light scratches on the paintwork, particularly on the wings and roof.

Jet-wash

The jet-wash at your local fuel station is easy to use – you merely choose how many minutes of washing time you want to buy, and insert tokens or a code. As a general guide, you'll need at least six minutes, more if you don't want to have to run around the car! Jet-washes are particularly good for removing stubborn dirt and mud, and you can blast muck off underneath the car too. Don't wear your best clothes though, as there's a chance you'll get wet, and possibly dirty. Most of these machines have a number of settings and tools. The machines differ in detail and operation, but as a general rule, begin by using the hot-water function with the high-pressure lance to wet the car and dislodge the dirt. Next, use the foam button to soap the car with shampoo. You can then use the soft soap brush provided to clean the dirt off. Don't forget to clean the wheels. Finally, rinse the car with the high-pressure lance using the wax function.

Hand washing

Often, the most satisfying and therapeutic way to clean your car – and certainly the cheapest – is to use the old-fashioned bucket-and-sponge method.

Firstly, rinse the car with water. Ideally, use a hose to do this (as long as there's no hose-pipe ban!). If you don't have a hose, just use a bucket of water with a sponge. Next, rinse the bucket out and refill with clean, warm water, then add car shampoo according to the instructions on the bottle. Don't be tempted to use more shampoo than recommended, as it can take forever to wash off, and can leave streaks. Never use household washing-up liquid, as its salt content is not good for the paintwork and can accelerate corrosion. Using the sponge, work around the car, removing all the dirt, not forgetting the wheels. Lift the windscreen wipers away from the screen to make life easier, and wipe the rubbers clean.

Once the car is clean and shiny, rinse once again with clean water. To prevent streaks on the paintwork it's then a good idea to dry the car with a chamois leather or micro-fibre cloth.

Polishing

To finish the process and to make your car gleam, a polish can be applied. Most modern polishes contain wax or silicone, which will provide a protective layer on the paintwork. Not only will this make the car sparkle, it will also protect the paintwork, keep it clean for longer, and make the cleaning process easier. Buy a good-quality polish – ask friends or the staff in your local car accessory shop for recommendations.

You'll need two polishing cloths – one to apply the polish, and one to remove it. It's best to polish your car in overcast weather, as bright sunlight can dry the polish quickly and can make it very hard to remove. Most polishes are applied to a dry car with a dry cloth, but follow the directions on the packaging.

Start in one corner of the car, applying the polish, using a soft cloth in a swirling motion, so it forms a thin film. You may want to polish one panel at a time, or you can apply polish to the whole car and then work around from the beginning to buff it off. You can tell when the polish is dry, as it will leave a powdery-like substance. Using the other clean cloth, remove the polish, again using a circular polishing motion, until the paintwork is gleaming. If the cloths become overloaded with polish that they have absorbed, discard them and use fresh ones.

Ensure you also clean the windows. You may be able to clean all the glass except for the windscreen itself with the polish too, but check the packaging, as many types are unsuitable for use on glass. As a rule, it's better to use a specialist glass cleaner, especially on the windscreen. Don't forget to clean the inside of the windscreen and windows, and your wing mirrors too.

Removing stubborn marks from bodywork

Bird droppings can be a particular problem, and can cause damage to paintwork due to their acid content. Droppings are best removed as soon as you notice them, even if you're not cleaning the rest of the car. The best way to do this is to soak a rag or some kitchen roll with water, and cover the droppings for a few minutes to soften them before gently wiping away. Don't be tempted to try and use anything abrasive, such as a kitchen scourer, as this will do far more damage to the paint than the droppings!

If the wheels are particularly dirty and difficult to clean, you can buy specialist wheel cleaner. Apply this with a stiff brush, such as an old washing-up brush, but make sure you wear gloves, as the chemicals in the cleaner are usually not good for your skin. An old toothbrush is also useful for those hard-to-reach areas, particularly on alloy wheels. Leave the solution on for a few minutes, as directed on the bottle, and then rinse off. You should then have sparkling wheels! To add a finishing touch, you can also buy tyre-shine products for that perfect look.

If you notice stubborn tar marks, or traffic film, again you can buy special products to remove these. Once the car has been washed, most marks of this type can be removed with a good-quality silicone polish and a little elbow grease!

Interior cleaning

When maintaining the interior of your car, prevention is better than cure – regular cleaning and tidying will prevent the need for major decontamination!

Removing stains from the interior

It goes without saying that stains are best dealt with as soon as they happen, but if one does catch you by surprise, here are some tips for their removal:

* **General stains** – on cloth upholstery or carpets, can often be dealt with using the same stain-removal products designed for use on carpets and clothes in the home. Always use these products according to the instructions provided.
* **Chewing gum** – is particularly difficult to remove – try running an ice cube over it to make it more brittle, and then scrape off.
* **Pet hair** – try a stiff brush or a sticky lint roller to remove as much hair as possible before vacuuming.
* **Milk** – can be the hardest stain, and smell, to remove. Clean up as much as you can, and then sprinkle the affected area with bicarbonate-of-soda. Leave for a few hours, or preferably overnight, then vacuum. If this fails, try mixing the bicarbonate-of-soda to a paste in a small dish, and then scrubbing it in to the stain. Again, leave overnight to dry, and then vacuum up. If all else fails, you may well need the attention of a professional valeter with wet-vac facilities and specialist chemicals.

Bicarbonate-of-soda can also be used to remove general odours. Sprinkle over carpets and upholstery, then leave overnight before vacuuming up thoroughly the following day.

To vacuum your car, it's best to use the vacuum cleaner you use in your house, as many of the budget hand-held car vacs are not powerful enough to do a good job. Begin with the seats, making a mental note of any stains you see so that you can return to them later. The crevice tool is great for reaching down beside and under the seats, and other difficult-to-reach areas where dirt tends to accumulate.

If you don't already have car mats, consider investing in some, as they are a great help in keeping the carpets clean – especially in wet weather – and make the job of cleaning quicker and easier. It's best to remove the mats to clean them – if they're made of rubber or plastic, clean them with soapy water before buffing with suitable trim or plastic cleaner. If the mats are fabric, give them a good shake (well away from the car), then vacuum. Don't forget to vacuum the boot too.

Next, clean the dashboard and other interior trim, such as door trims, arm rests etc. These areas can be cleaned with a damp cloth, but for a better finish, specialist cleaners can be used. Most of these cleaners have the added advantage of keeping your car smelling nice and fresh. Plastic and vinyl cleaners often come in a choice of matt or gloss finish. Apply the cleaner to a cloth first, then use the cloth to buff the trim. It's advisable to avoid using these cleaners on the steering wheel, handbrake lever and gear lever, as this can make them slippery and hence dangerous.

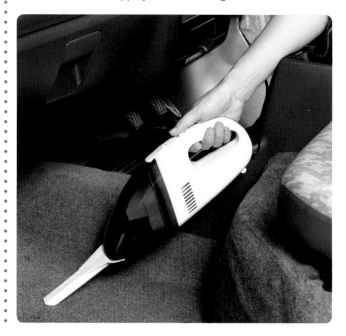

Paint and bodywork repairs

If your car has major damage to its bodywork and/or paintwork, then this is probably a job best left to the professionals. However, there are many minor repairs that you can carry out yourself, which will both save you money and give you the satisfaction that you fixed it yourself and didn't need to take the car to a bodyshop!

Faded or dull paintwork

If you have an older car, you may well notice that the paintwork has become dull or faded. This often happens with older cars painted a 'solid' colour – ie, not metallic or pearlescent paint. With solid paints, which do not have a layer of lacquer sprayed over the top, the pigments in the paint can become affected by exposure to sunlight in a process known as oxidisation. Red is the most susceptible colour to this, but it does happen to other colours. As long as the paint hasn't deteriorated too far, you can often revive the colour using a colour restorer. A wide range of paint-restoration products is available, and some are coloured for use on a specific paint colour. All are mildly abrasive, and work by removing a thin layer of paint, so care must be taken!

Here are a few tips on how to use paint restoration products:

1 It's best to start off with a restorer that's only mildly abrasive. Paint is easy to take off, but you can't put it back on! Try the restorer out on a small area first, to see what the results will be like, before you start on a large panel – don't rub too hard, as some products remove paint very quickly.

2 You'll need plenty of soft cloths. Use separate cloths for applying the colour restorer and for buffing-off, changing the cloths as they become covered with paint. Cotton cloths are best, to avoid the problem of particles of cloth sticking to the paint as you work.

3 Once you're satisfied with the results, apply a coat of good-quality polish to the whole car. Ideally, use a polish with added UV protection to block the sun's rays and help prolong the life of your car's shiny paintwork.

Sometimes, a paint finish with a clear (lacquer) coat can deteriorate too, and the clear coat can start to lift off, although this is rare. There's a variation on this problem where air gets in between the clear coat and the base paint, oxidising the paint. This appears as a white, blotchy layer under the clear coat. Unfortunately, there's no easy fix for either of these problems – the only long-term fix is to have the affected area professionally re-sprayed.

Removing light scratches and swirls

Scratches which haven't completely penetrated the paint layer, and swirl marks caused by car washes, can normally be removed – or at least made less visible – by using a special paint-cutting compound. This is available in most car accessory shops. The compound contains tiny, grit-like particles that act like a very fine abrasive paper and remove paint to create a smooth surface. For this reason, they should be used very carefully – if you take off too much paint, you'll soon reach the base layer and the panel will need re-spraying.

To use this compound, apply a pea-sized drop of compound to a soft cloth, and rub on and around the scratch. After a couple of minutes, wipe the area clean and assess the result. Repeat the process until the scratch has disappeared, or significantly faded, then use a polish to buff to a shine.

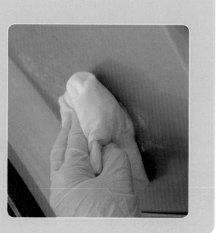

Touching up paint

If you notice a chip or a scratch when you're cleaning your car, it's best to touch it in as soon as you can, before it starts to rust or fill with dirt, and develops into a more serious problem.

CHOOSING THE RIGHT TOUCH-UP PAINT

Every car has a paint code, which is marked on the car when it's painted at the factory. If you're going to buy paint from a car manufacturer's approved parts department, take your car along – the staff will know where to find the code, often on a plate under the bonnet, or a sticker in the door shut or the boot. Car accessory shops also sell touch-up paint, and as long as you have the paint code, they may even be able to mix to order if they don't have your colour in stock.

You can usually buy touch-up paint in two forms – easy-to-use 'touch-up sticks', or spray cans. The stick consists of a small canister of paint, with a brush built into the lid.

If your car has a two-coat finish, with a clear top-coat, you should be supplied with two paint sticks, or spray cans, in a kit – one stick, or can, containing the colour coat, and the other the clear coat.

USING TOUCH-UP PAINT

Firstly, bear in mind that touching up a small chip or scratch using a touch-up stick is a straightforward job, but using a spray can is an entirely different proposition, because to spray successfully you need to mask surrounding areas to prevent overspray. For best results, you need to spray inside a well-ventilated garage, or at least away from any wind or draughts. It's also important to keep the spray nozzle clean all the time you're spraying. A detailed procedure for spray-painting isn't included here, because it could be a whole book in itself, but here's a guide to touching up using a touch-up stick:

1 Carefully clean around the affected area. It's best to use plain water, without car shampoo or any additives – anything else might damage the paintwork, or stop the new paint sticking. Let the paintwork dry fully.

2 Using the small wire brush supplied with some touch-up sticks, or a piece of emery paper or wire wool, carefully remove any rust from the chip or scratch. Try not to damage surrounding paintwork (wrapping wire wool round the end of a pencil helps).

3 The paint must be thoroughly mixed, usually by shaking the touch-up stick for a few minutes – follow the instructions. Apply a small amount of paint, using the touch-up stick brush or, better still, a very fine artist's brush. Work slowly, and brush one way. Try to 'fill' the scratch, and don't let the new paint build up higher than the good paint around the scratch. With a two-coat finish, follow the instructions and apply the clear coat after the colour coat has dried.

4 Wait a few days for the paint to dry completely, then rub the painted area using a polishing compound (or a very mild abrasive colour restorer) to blend in the new paint. Once you're happy with the result, wash and polish the car to finish off.

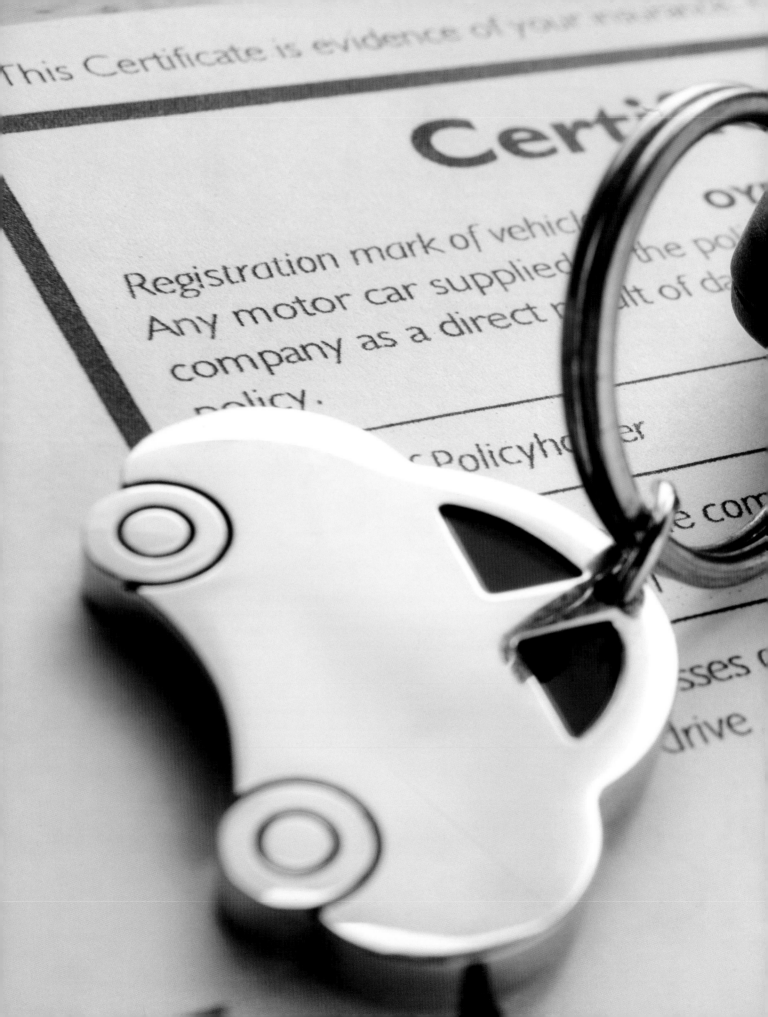

PAPERWORK

Modern life seems to be awash with paperwork, and your car is no exception. The necessary paperwork for a car can seem quite complicated, and this is not helped by the fact that documents are often referred to by more than one name – their official name and an adopted one. An example of this is a car's registration document – often officially referred to as the 'V5C', but also known as the 'logbook'.

Much of the paperwork for your car is a legal requirement, and you may need to produce certain items if you're involved in an accident or are stopped by the police for any reason. Keeping your paperwork up to date and in one place will make life a lot easier. It's also worth keeping a record of the expiry dates of your car's tax, MoT and insurance, so you don't end up inadvertently driving illegally.

As a driver you must have:
* A valid driving licence.
* A valid certificate of insurance.

Your car must also have:
* A vehicle registration document.
* Road tax.
* A current MoT.

In addition to these items, there are other items you may have for the vehicle, that also need to be kept in a safe place:
* Service record book.
* Breakdown cover policy.
* Warranty policy.
* Car handbook, and instruction booklets for items such as sound system, sat nav, child seats, etc.
* Old invoices and warranties for any work carried out, such as a new exhaust or tyres, including those you may have inherited with the car (these will be useful if you come to sell the car, and might increase its value and saleability).

DRIVING LICENCE

You must have both the photo-card and counterpart of your licence, and you may be required to produce these if you have a crash or get stopped by the police. The paper part of your licence is normally valid until you are 70. However, the photo-card expires every ten years. Many people are unaware of this, and if you get caught, at the time of writing, the penalty is a fine of up to £1,000, so it's worth checking the validity of your licence. Large numbers of people also forget to get their licence updated when they move home, or change their name when they get married. Again, having incorrect details carries a penalty of up to £1,000, updating it is free and you can do it online via the DVLA website.

INSURANCE

You must have a valid insurance certificate to drive any car that you're using. Being caught without insurance is a serious offence, and can result in six penalty points on your licence, a nasty fine,

and confiscation of the vehicle in question. It's your responsibility to check that you're insured, so if a friend lends you their car and swears blind you are covered to drive on their insurance, you'll still be prosecuted if it turns out that you're not covered after all.

It's a legal requirement to insure your car before you drive it on the road, but since June 2011 you must also insure it even if it's just parked in the garage or on your drive. The exception to this is if you officially declare the car as being kept off the road and not used, by completing a SORN (Statutory Off-Road Notice) and sending it to DVLA, either online at their website, or by filling in a V890 form, which you can obtain at most post offices. If you've declared a SORN for your vehicle, it does not need to be insured or taxed, and does not need an MoT certificate.

The responsibility for ensuring that the car is insured lies with the registered keeper – the person whose name is on the registration document. This is usually, but not always, the vehicle owner.

VEHICLE REGISTRATION DOCUMENT (V5C)

By law, every vehicle must have a registration document, which shows the registered keeper of the vehicle. The keeper is the person who keeps the vehicle on a public road, and is responsible for making sure it's taxed, has a valid MoT and is insured, as well as being responsible for dealing with any penalty notices such as parking or speeding tickets. The registered keeper is usually, but not always, the legal owner of the vehicle.

The registration document gives the keeper's name and address and the registration number of the vehicle. It also gives other information about the vehicle, such as the date it was first registered, the Vehicle Identification Number (VIN), engine number, colour, engine size, body type, etc. The number of previous keepers is usually shown too.

The document also includes sections that must be filled in when a vehicle is sold, both by the buyer and by the seller. If you sell a car, it's your responsibility to send off the V5C to DVLA to inform them of the new keeper – the new owner retains the 'new keeper' section until he or she receives a new V5C. The only exception to this is when you sell to a motor trader – in this case you remove and fill in the yellow slip 'selling to a motor trader', which you post to DVLA, and the rest of the V5C is given to the motor

trader. You will also need to inform DVLA if you make any major changes to the car, such as altering its colour. Again, there is a slip for this. Instructions, and the appropriate address to which the paperwork must be sent, are given on the back of the registration document.

VEHICLE EXCISE LICENCE (TAX)

Vehicle tax was originally introduced way back in 1888, and from 1921 it became a legal requirement to display a valid tax disc. This tradition continued for almost 100 years, before the tax disc was finally scrapped on 1 October 2014.

As with many things, vehicle licensing is now fully computerised. You can buy tax online, or at a post office, to last for six or twelve months, or you can register to pay monthly.

For cars registered before 1 March 2001, the rate of tax depends on the engine size – cars with an engine up to 1,549cc are eligible for a cheaper rate. For cars registered after 1 March 2001, the rate depends on the level of carbon dioxide (CO_2) emissions – the less CO_2 the engine produces, the lower the tax rate.

It's worth noting that cars built (not necessarily registered) before 1 January 1973 are considered to be 'classics', and there's no charge for tax, although you'll still need to apply.

MOT CERTIFICATE

All cars need an MoT test when they reach three years old, and every year from then onwards. The only exceptions to this are vehicles built before 1960, which are exempt from the test.

The MoT test consists of a number of checks to ensure that your car is roadworthy – see Chapter 5 for more details. Since 2006, all MoT records have been computerised, and when your car obtains that all-important pass, you'll receive a black-and-white MoT certificate printed on plain paper, which states that it's a receipt, as all records are held on the VOSA computer. The advantages of this are that the police can easily check that your car has a valid MoT, a new certificate is easy to obtain should you lose it, and fraud/forgery is almost impossible.

You can have your car tested up to one month before the current certificate runs out – the expiry date of the new certificate will be 12 months after the date of expiry of the old one.

The MoT certificate shows details of the car, including the registration number and Vehicle Identification Number (VIN), the mileage recorded when the test was carried out, and the mileage recorded on the previous three certificates. This mileage history is an attempt to stamp out 'clocking' (illegally changing the vehicle mileage to show fewer miles than the car has actually covered). The MoT certificate will also show where the vehicle was tested, and who carried out the test, along with the date and time of issue, and the expiry date.

It's illegal to drive a car on the road without a valid MoT, and may invalidate your insurance.

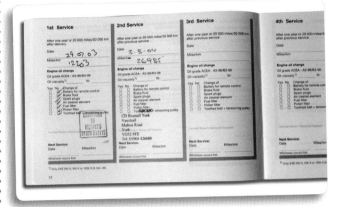

SERVICE RECORDS

When a car is new, it comes with a service record book, which shows details of all the scheduled servicing recommended by the manufacturer. Spaces are provided so that the garage carrying out servicing can stamp the book and write in the mileage and date. Although there's no legal requirement to keep this book, or even to have it stamped, it does provide a record to prove that the car has been serviced in line with the manufacturer's recommended schedule. It will often also show when other items have been replaced, such as the clutch or timing belt. This service record book can be very useful when you're buying or selling a car, because as long as it contains the official stamps of the garages that carried out the servicing, it shows that the car has been properly serviced. Cars with a 'full service history' tend to sell for a better price than those without.

Some owners keep all the invoices and receipts for servicing and other repairs. These can be useful when you sell the car, as this paperwork provides more evidence that the car has been well maintained.

OTHER PAPERWORK

Any other paperwork relating to your car, such as instructions, finance agreement, warranty schedule, or breakdown cover policy, should also be kept safe. However, you may like to keep the owner's handbook in the car in case you need to refer to it. If you have breakdown cover, also ensure that you have your policy number and the emergency telephone number to hand in the car. Breakdown companies often provide these details on a card for you to keep in a safe place.

BUYING AND SELLING A CAR

When you set out to buy a car, there is now a huge and often bewildering array of types and models to choose from and it can be a daunting task to narrow your selection down to just one or two, let alone actually buy one! As a woman, the experience can also feel intimidating.

Selling your car can be a somewhat daunting prospect, whether it's a private sale or a part-exchange, but it really doesn't need to be. If you remember a few simple things, you shouldn't encounter any serious problems.

Buying a car

Even after you've decided what type of car you would like to buy, there are many things to consider. Where to buy, what questions to ask, how to finance the purchase, what price you should expect to pay, warranties and, if you're buying a used car, how to spot a dodgy car or rogue trader.

The internet is great for information, although it can sometimes be a minefield, and once you've narrowed your choice down to a few models, there are numerous forums you can visit for information on drivability, reliability and just about anything else you'd like to know. Just search for the make and model of car you're interested in, and you'll find huge amounts of information, often in the form of angry customers moaning about their cars! This information is well worth reading, as there are big differences in customer satisfaction between different manufacturers, and some models have common faults.

FUEL TYPE

Another thing to consider is fuel type. Petrol cars tend to be cheaper to buy, but often the fuel consumption is poorer than a

diesel equivalent, although modern technology has seen petrol-engine economy improve quite dramatically in the last few years. Be aware though, that it's not a good idea to buy a modern diesel with a diesel particulate filter (DPF) if you intend to use it only for short journeys. This is because the filter needs to reach high temperatures to keep itself clean, and this won't happen if you only do short journeys. If the filter gets blocked and fails, it could result in an expensive bill to replace it. One way to avoid this is to go for, say, a 20-minute drive at 70mph (110kph) on a dual-carriageway or motorway once a week to get the filter hot.

LPG (Liquid Petroleum Gas) is another fuel option, either factory-fitted, or as an aftermarket kit. This can offer significant savings, particularly on large and thirsty engines, however some people do report a slight drop in performance.

Electric cars have also started to become available, but these are expensive to buy, and most have a relatively short range between charges.

BUDGET AND DEPRECIATION

If you're buying a new car, consider also that depreciation will mean that it's worth considerably less than you paid for it as soon as you drive it off the forecourt, and after three years it will be worth on average only 40 per cent of what you paid for it – so on a £15,000 car, you would have lost £9,000 – ouch!

Depreciation has slowed considerably by the time a car is around five years old, and a budget of £2,000–£5,000 can buy you a great car with many years of happy motoring left in it.

Once a car is over eight years old, it has done most of the depreciation it's going to do. This is generally the 'budget' end of the market, but there are plenty of cars costing less that £2,000 that can still provide reliable and enjoyable motoring. Obviously though, this is an area in which to be very careful. Also bear in mind that maintenance and repair costs on an older car can be considerably higher than those for a newer car.

FINANCE

So you've decided on your budget and, assuming you're not lucky enough to have the money sitting in your bank account, then there are a number of funding options to consider. If you're buying from a main dealer, they will be very keen to offer you finance, as they

usually get a fat commission for doing so. The same can be said of buying a used car from an independent dealer. If you're considering taking this route, be careful – don't allow the salesman to pressure you, and read the small-print carefully. If you're at all unsure, ask for a copy of the finance agreement and take it away to look at, and possibly get a second opinion. Don't be fooled by the 'it's a today only' sales tactic. It's one of the many common 'lines' to get you to sign up there and then.

Approaching your bank manager for a chat about a loan can be a useful idea, and if you have a sympathetic manager, he or she may also be able to offer you some helpful advice about other forms of credit. As with all loans though, read the small-print carefully and check that you'll be able to comfortably afford the repayments.

Credit cards are also a possibility, but be particularly wary when considering this option. Unless you have a long, zero-per-cent or low-interest deal, don't even consider it, as the interest you will have to pay could be ridiculously high.

Many first cars are bought by part or full finance from a relative, usually Mum or Dad, and older purchasers will still often turn to family or sometimes friends to help out, particularly on lower-priced used cars. This can work well, provided everybody knows the terms of the deal!

PRIVATE, DEALER OR AUCTION?

Obviously, a new car will be bought from a main dealer, but in the used market you have the choice of buying privately, or from a dealer. A private purchase will usually get you a better deal, and you'll get more car for your money. However, you don't have as many rights when you buy from a private individual – the seller only

has to describe the car correctly in the advert, and they are not responsible for any faults.

Buying from a trader is more expensive, but provides you with much more protection. Under the Sale of Goods Act 1979, you can

expect a car to be of satisfactory quality taking in to consideration the price you have paid, the age of the car, and the mileage. The law recognises that a second-hand car won't be perfect, but it must be fit for use on the road, reasonably reliable and safe, and in a condition that reflects its age and price. It must also be 'fit for purpose'. The mileage must be correct unless it has been disclaimed (or not warranted), in which case walk away from the deal, and the car must match any written or verbal description given. Most importantly, if a car is faulty, you have rights which exist automatically between you and the trader. Any guarantee or warranty given by the trader will be in addition to these rights.

Remember also that you have the same rights buying from a dealer on his driveway as you do buying from a main agent or large independent trader.

Buying from an auction can be a very risky process, and not to be recommended for the novice purchaser! Many cars sold at auction are 'sold as seen', which means that the seller and auction house accept no responsibility if there's anything wrong with the car. Even traders who purchase from auction have been known to get their fingers burned. There are bargains to be had, particularly if you're an experienced buyer, but buying at auction can be a risk for the unwary.

Wherever you decide to buy from, where possible take a friend with you – even if they have no more knowledge than you, it can be helpful to have moral support. Always insist on a test drive and, with a used car, listen for any nasty noises such as clonks, rattles and knocks. Also ask about the car's history, including service history, MoT records and any repairs.

Take a walk around the car, checking for damage, and ask to see under the bonnet. Even if you don't know what you're looking

at, a clean and tidy engine compartment often reflects the fact that the car has been well maintained.

Feel free to ask any other questions you feel relevant, and if you feel at all uncomfortable, walk away – it's your money, and there are lots more cars out there!

Selling a car

The first thing to do when selling your car is find out how much it's worth. For a private sale you should expect to charge a private retail value, which will be less than a trader would charge. If you're part-exchanging, or if you're simply selling your car to a garage, then you should expect a trade value (around 60 per cent of retail price in most cases).

There are several ways to find your car's retail value. The cheapest way is to look at a few online car-sales sites. In most cases there will be similar cars to yours for sale. Check cars that have a slightly lower and slightly higher mileage than your own, to give you an accurate picture. Once you're happy you're in the right price range, set your own price, but remember to consider the lowest price you would accept for the car and add about ten per cent for negotiation.

If you're selling privately, once you've decided on the value of your car, you'll need to prepare it for sale. It may seem obvious, but still worth bearing in mind, that a car with at least a few months' MoT and tax will be worth more, and will be a lot easier to sell, than one without.

Once you're happy that your car is ready for sale, you now need to decide how you would like to sell it. Either online, in a newspaper or local magazine, or even just on your drive with a 'For Sale' sign.

Probably the best way to reach a large number of potential buyers is by advertising online using one of the various car-sales websites – costs can vary, although some sites are free for private sellers.

Once you have someone interested, they are likely to ask lots of questions, so make sure you're prepared. Common questions include:

* How many miles has the car done?
* Has it got full service history, and when was it last serviced?
* How many owners has the car had?
* When does the MoT and tax run out?
* When was the timing belt (cam belt) last changed?

With a little patience, and perhaps an element of good luck, you should soon have customers lining up to view your pride and joy!

APPENDICES

Glossary

Useful contacts

Glossary

The following guide is intended to help you to understand some of the more common terms that you'll come across when discussing your car with your local garage, or when talking to the local pub-bore!

ABS – Anti-lock Braking System. Uses sensors at each wheel to sense when the wheels are about to lock, and releases the brakes to prevent locking.

Air bag – An inflatable bag that inflates in the event of a sudden impact, to protect the driver and/or passengers from injury. Driver's air bags are usually mounted in the steering wheel and passenger's air bags are usually mounted in the dashboard. Some cars also have side-impact air bags, which may be mounted in various different locations.

Air conditioning – A system that enables the temperature of the air inside the car to be lowered, and dehumidifies the air. This allows more comfort and rapid demisting.

Air filter – A renewable paper or foam filter that removes foreign particles from the air that are sucked into the engine.

Airflow sensor – A sensor used in an engine management system to measure the amount of air being sucked into the engine.

Alternator – An electrical generator driven by the engine. It provides electricity for the car's electrical system when the engine's running, and to charge the battery.

Antifreeze – A fluid that's added to water to produce engine coolant. The antifreeze stops the coolant freezing in cold weather, and prevents corrosion inside the engine.

Anti-roll bar – A metal bar used in front and/or rear suspension systems to reduce the tendency of the car's body to roll from side to side. Not all cars have them.

Balljoint – A maintenance-free flexible joint used mainly in suspension and steering systems to allow for movement of the components. Consists of a metal ball and cup, with a rubber seal to retain the grease.

Battery – A 'reservoir' that stores electricity. Provides the power to start the engine, and power for the electrical systems when the engine's stopped, and is charged by the alternator when the engine's running.

Bearing – A metal or other hard-wearing surface against which another part moves, and which is designed to reduce friction and wear. A bearing is usually lubricated.

Big-end – The lower end of a connecting rod which connects a piston to the engine's crankshaft. It incorporates a bearing, and transmits the movement of the connecting rod to the crankshaft.

Bleed nipple (or valve) – A screw, usually hollow, which allows fluid or air to be bled out of a system when it's loosened.

Bore – A term used to describe the diameter of a cylinder in an engine.

Brake bleeding – A procedure for removing air from the brake hydraulic system.

Brake caliper – The part of a disc brake system that houses the brake pads and the hydraulic pistons. The caliper straddles the brake disc.

Brake disc – A rotating metal disc coupled to a roadwheel, which is clamped between two brake pads in a disc brake system. As the brake disc slows down due to friction, so does the roadwheel.

Brake drum – A rotating metal drum coupled to a roadwheel. The brake shoes rub on the inside of the drum. As the brake drum slows down due to friction, so does the roadwheel.

Brake fade – A temporary reduction in braking power due to overheating of the brake friction material.

Brake fluid – A hydraulic fluid resistant to high temperatures, used in hydraulic braking systems and some hydraulic clutch systems.

Brake pad – A metal plate, with a pad of hard-wearing friction material bonded to one side. When the brakes are applied the hydraulic pistons in the brake caliper push the pads against the brake disc.

Brake servo – A vacuum-operated device that increases the force applied to the brake master cylinder by the brake pedal. Vacuum is supplied from the inlet manifold on a petrol engine, or from a vacuum pump on a diesel engine.

Brake shoe – A curved metal former with friction material bonded to the outside surface. When the brakes are applied the hydraulic pistons in the wheel cylinder push the brake shoes against the brake drum.

Breather – An opening or valve that allows air or fumes out of a system, or fresh air into a system.

Bump stop – A hard piece of rubber or plastic used in many suspension systems to prevent the moving parts from touching the body during suspension movements.

Caliper – See Brake caliper.

Cam belt – See Timing belt.

Camshaft – A rotating shaft driven from the crankshaft, with lobes or cams used to operate the valves, via the valve gear.

Camshaft sensor – A sensor used in an engine management system to provide information on the position of the camshaft.

Carburettor – A device that's used to mix air and petrol in the correct proportions required for burning by the engine. Superseded on modern cars by fuel injection systems.

Catalytic converter – A device fitted in the exhaust system that reduces the amount of harmful gases released into the atmosphere.

Clutch – A friction device that allows two separate rotating components to be coupled together smoothly, without the need for either rotating component to stop moving.

Coil – See Ignition coil.

Coil spring – A spiral coil of sprung steel used in many suspension systems.

Combustion chamber – Shaped area into which the air/fuel mixture is compressed by the piston, and where the mixture is ignited. The combustion chamber may be formed in the cylinder head, or sometimes in the top of the piston.

Connecting rod (con rod) – A metal rod in the engine connecting a piston to the crankshaft. The connecting rod transfers the up-and-down motion of the piston to the crankshaft.

Constant velocity (CV) joint – A joint used in drive shafts where the speed of the input shaft is exactly the same as the speed of the output shaft no matter what the angle of the joint.

Coolant – A liquid consisting of a mixture of water and antifreeze, used in a car's engine cooling system.

Coolant (water) pump – A pump driven by the engine that pumps the coolant around the cooling system.

Cooling fan – Electric or engine-driven fan mounted at the front of the engine compartment and designed to cool the radiator.

CPS (Crankshaft Position Sensor) – A sensor used in an engine management system to provide information on the position and/or speed of the crankshaft.

Crankcase – The area of the cylinder block below the pistons, which houses the crankshaft.

Crankshaft – A cranked metal shaft that translates the up-and-down motion of the pistons and connecting rods into rotary motion.

CTS (Coolant Temperature Sensor) – A sensor used in an engine management system, or possibly in several other systems to provide information on the temperature of the engine coolant.

CV joint – See Constant velocity joint.

CVT – Continuously Variable Transmission. An automatic transmission with no fixed gear ratios. The gear ratios are constantly varied using a system of conical pulleys and a drive belt.

Cylinder – A metal tube in the engine, in which a piston slides. The cylinders may be bored directly into the cylinder block, or cylinder liners may be fitted.

Cylinder block – The main engine casting, which houses the cylinders, crankshaft, pistons and connecting rods.

Cylinder head – The casting at the top of the engine that houses the valves and associated components. The cylinder head is bolted to the cylinder block.

Cylinder head gasket – A gasket fitted to provide a leak-proof seal between an engine's cylinder block and cylinder head.

Damper – See Shock absorber.

Depreciation – The reduction in value of a car as time passes.

Diagnostic light (engine warning light) – A warning light on the instrument panel that illuminates when a fault code has been stored in the engine electronic control unit memory.

Diesel engine – an engine that relies on the heat produced when air is compressed to ignite the fuel, and so doesn't need an ignition system. Diesel engines have a much higher compression ratio than petrol engines.

Differential – A system of gears which provides drive to two wheels, but allows the wheels to turn at different speeds, for example during cornering.

Dipstick – A metal or plastic rod with graduated marks used to check the level of a fluid.

Distributor – A device used to distribute the ignition HT circuit current to the individual spark plugs. The distributor may also control the ignition timing.

Distributor cap – A plastic cap that fits on top of the distributor, inside which the rotor arm rotates to distribute the HT circuit current to the correct spark plug. The cap contains electrodes (one for each cylinder).

Drive belt – A belt, usually made from rubber, used to transmit drive between two pulleys or sprockets. Often used to drive the camshafts and engine ancillaries.

Drive shaft – Term used to describe a shaft that transmits drive from a differential to one wheel.

Drum brake – See Brake drum.

Earth strap – A flexible electrical connection between the battery and the car's body, or between the engine/transmission and the body, to provide an electrical earth return to the battery.

EBD – Electronic Brakeforce Distribution. An electronically controlled braking system that ensures the braking force is distributed evenly between all four wheels to keep the car stable when braking. Usually combined with the ABS system.

ECU – Electronic Control Unit. A unit that receives electrical inputs from various sensors, processes the inputs, and produces electrical outputs to control one or more actuators.

EFI – Electronic Fuel Injection.

EGR – Exhaust Gas Recirculation. An emissions control system that recirculates a proportion of the exhaust gases back into the engine, where they are burnt with fresh air/fuel mixture.

Electrode – An electrical terminal, eg, in a spark plug or distributor cap.

Electrolyte – A solution of sulphuric acid and distilled water that conducts electrical current in a battery.

Emissions – Harmful substances (gases or particles) released into the atmosphere from a car's systems (usually the exhaust, fuel system or engine breather system).

Emissions control – A method of reducing the emissions released into the atmosphere. Various different systems are used.

Engine management system – A system that uses an electronic control unit to control the operation of the ignition system and fuel injection system, improving engine efficiency and reducing emissions.

Engine warning light – See Diagnostic light.

EVAP – An emissions control system on petrol-engined cars which stores vapour from the fuel tank and then releases it to be burnt, along with fresh mixture, by the engine.

Exhaust manifold – A device used for ducting the exhaust gases from the engine's cylinder head into the exhaust system.

Expansion tank – A container used in many cars' cooling systems to collect the overflow from the system as the coolant heats up and expands. Usually combined with the coolant reservoir.

Fan belt – Another term for a drive belt. The name arose because on older cars a drive belt was used to drive the cooling fan. Electric cooling fans are used on most modern cars.

Fault code – An electronic code stored in the memory of an electronic control unit which gives details of a fault detected by the self-diagnostic system. A diagnostic light on the instrument panel will usually illuminate to indicate a fault.

Fault code reader – An electronic tool used to translate fault codes into a form that indicates where the fault lies.

Feeler gauges/blades – Thin strips of metal of a measured thickness used to check clearances between components, such as a spark plug gap.

Final drive – Another term used to describe a differential assembly.

Flywheel – A heavy metal disc attached to one end of the crankshaft in an engine, used to smooth out the power pulses from the pistons.

Four-stroke – A term used to describe the four operating strokes of a piston in a car engine.

Free play – The 'slack' in a linkage or an assembly of parts – for example, the distance the brake pedal moves before the master cylinder is actuated.

Friction disc – A metal disc with friction material attached to both sides used in a clutch assembly to progressively couple two rotating components together.

FSH – Full Service History. A written record which shows that a car has been serviced from new in accordance with the manufacturer's recommendations.

Fuel filter – A renewable filter that removes foreign particles from the fuel.

Fuel injection – A method of injecting a measured amount of fuel into an engine.

Fuel injection pump – A device that controls the quantity of fuel delivered to the fuel injectors in a diesel engine, and also controls the instant at which the injectors inject fuel.

Fuel injector – A device used to inject fuel into an engine. Some engines use a single fuel injector, whilst some use one fuel injector for each cylinder.

Fuel pressure regulator – A device that controls the pressure of the fuel delivered to the fuel injectors in a petrol fuel injection engine.

Fuel pump – A device that pumps fuel from the fuel tank to the fuel system.

Gasket – A compressible material used between two surfaces to give a leak-proof joint.

Gearbox – A group of gears and shafts in a housing used to keep a car's engine within its safe operating speed range as the speed of the car changes.

Glow plug – An electrical heating device fitted to a diesel engine to help it start from cold, and to reduce the smoke produced immediately after start-up. Each cylinder usually has its own glow plug.

Head gasket – See Cylinder head gasket.

Heater matrix – A small radiator mounted in the engine's coolant circuit that provides hot air for the car's heating system. Hot coolant flows through the matrix, which heats the surrounding air.

HT (high tension) circuit – The electrical circuit containing the high voltage used to fire the spark plugs in an ignition system.

HT (high tension) leads – Electrical leads which carry the HT circuit voltage to the spark plugs.

Hydraulic – A term used to describe the operation of a component or system by means of fluid pressure.

Hydraulic lifter (or tappet) – A valve lifter where the valve clearance is taken up hydraulically using oil pressure. This eliminates the need for valve clearance adjustment.

Idle speed – The running speed of an engine when the throttle is closed – ie, when the car is at rest and the driver isn't pressing the accelerator pedal.

Ignition coil – An electrical coil that generates the HT circuit voltage in a petrol engine ignition system to fire the spark plugs.

Ignition system – The electrical system that controls the spark used to ignite the air/fuel mixture in a petrol engine.

Ignition timing – A measure of the instant in the cylinder firing cycle at which ignition spark (provided by the spark plug) occurs in a petrol engine. The firing point is usually a few degrees of crankshaft rotation before the piston reaches the top of its stroke.

Independent suspension – A suspension system where movement of one wheel has no effect on the movement of the other, eg, independent front suspension or independent rear suspension.

Indirect injection – A type of fuel injection system where the fuel is injected by a fuel injector into a swirl chamber (diesel engine) or the inlet manifold (petrol engine) before entering the combustion chamber.

Inertia reel – Automatic type of seatbelt mechanism that allows the wearer to move freely in normal use, but locks when the car decelerates suddenly or the wearer moves suddenly.

Injection timing – The instant in an engine's cylinder firing cycle at which fuel injection occurs.

Inlet manifold – A ducting, usually made of metal or plastic, which directs the air or air/fuel mixture into the engine's cylinder head.

Input shaft – The shaft that transmits drive from the clutch to the gearbox in a manual gearbox, or from the torque converter to the transmission in an automatic transmission.

Jump leads – Heavy electrical cables fitted with clamps to enable a car's battery to be connected to another battery for emergency starting.

Kickdown – A device used on an automatic transmission that allows a lower gear to be selected for improved acceleration by fully depressing the accelerator pedal.

Knocking (Pinking) – A metallic noise from the engine often caused by the ignition timing being incorrect or a build up of carbon inside the engine. The noise is due to pressure waves that cause the cylinder walls to vibrate.

Knock sensor – A sensor that senses the onset of knocking and sends an electrical signal to the engine management system, to enable the ignition timing to be adjusted to prevent it.

Lambda sensor – See Oxygen sensor.

Laminated windscreen – A windscreen that has a thin plastic layer sandwiched between two layers of toughened glass. It will not shatter or craze when hit.

Lean – A term used to describe an air/fuel mixture containing less than the optimum amount of fuel.

Locknut – A nut used to lock another threaded component in place to prevent it from working loose.

Lockwasher – A washer designed to prevent a nut or bolt from working loose.

LPG – Liquefied Petroleum Gas. A mixture of liquefied petroleum gases, such as propane and butane, which are obtained from crude oil. Used in some engines as an alternative to petrol and diesel fuel.

MacPherson strut – An independent suspension component, which combines a coil spring and a shock absorber so that the swivelling, springing and shock absorbing for a wheel is carried out by a single assembly.

MAP sensor – Manifold Absolute Pressure sensor. A sensor that measures the pressure in the inlet manifold of a petrol engine and sends an electrical signal to the engine management system.

MAF (Mass Airflow Sensor) – See Airflow sensor.

Master cylinder – A cylinder containing a piston and hydraulic fluid, directly coupled to a foot pedal (or brake servo). Used for transmitting fluid pressure to the brake or clutch operating mechanisms.

Mixture – The air/fuel mixture burnt by an

engine to produce power. In a petrol engine, the optimum ratio of air to fuel for complete combustion is 14.7:1.

Multi-point fuel injection – A fuel injection system that has one fuel injector for each cylinder of the engine.

Multi-valve – An engine with more than two valves per cylinder. Usually four valves per cylinder (two inlet and two exhaust valves), or sometimes three valves per cylinder (two inlet valves and one exhaust valve).

NOx – Oxides of Nitrogen. Toxic emissions found in the exhaust gases of petrol and diesel engines.

OBD – On-Board Diagnostics. A system that monitors the operation of the engine management system and records a fault code if any fault occurs within the system that may affect the exhaust emissions.

Octane rating – A scale rating for grading petrol. The higher the octane number, the more energy a given amount of petrol will produce when it's burnt by the engine.

OHC – OverHead Camshaft. An engine layout where the camshaft is mounted above the valves. Because the camshaft operates the valves directly (via the valve gear), an OHC engine is more efficient than an OHV engine.

OHV – OverHead Valve. An engine layout where the valves are located in the cylinder head, but the valve gear is operated by pushrods from a camshaft located lower in the cylinder block. Rare for modern engines.

Oil filter – A renewable filter that removes foreign particles from the engine oil.

O-ring – A type of sealing ring made of rubber. An O-ring is usually clamped between two surfaces (often into a groove) to provide a seal.

Overhead camshaft – See OHC.

Overhead valve – See OHV.

Oxygen sensor (O2 sensor) – Provides information on the amount of oxygen present in the exhaust gases. Used in a closed-loop catalytic converter system to enable the engine management system to control the air/fuel mixture.

PAS – Power-Assisted Steering. See Power steering.

Pinion – A term for a gear with a small number of teeth, which meshes with a gear having a larger number of teeth.

Pinking – See Knocking.

Piston – Cylindrical component which slides in a close-fitting cylinder. The pistons in an engine compress the air/fuel mixture, transmit power to the crankshaft via the connecting rods, and push the burnt gases out through the exhaust valves.

Piston ring – A hardened metal ring which spring-fits in a groove running around a piston. The piston ring ensures a gas-tight seal between the piston and the cylinder wall.

Power steering – A system that uses hydraulic pressure to provide assistance when the driver turns the steering wheel.

Pre-ignition – See Knocking.

Pressure cap – Acts as a cooling system safety valve by venting steam or hot coolant if the pressure rises above a certain level. Also acts as a vacuum relief valve to stop a vacuum forming in the system as it cools.

Propeller shaft – The shaft which transmits drive from the manual gearbox or automatic transmission to the differential on a front-engined, rear-wheel-drive car or to the rear and/or front differential on a four-wheel-drive car.

Pulse air – An emissions control system that introduces fresh air into the exhaust manifold through tubes, to raise the temperature of the exhaust gases. This in turn causes the catalytic converter to warm up more quickly.

Pushrods – Used on OHV engines (where the camshaft is mounted remotely from the valve gear) to operate the valve gear. The camshaft lobes act on the pushrods, which transfer the rotary movement of the camshaft lobes to the up-and-down movement required to operate the valves via the valve gear.

Rack-and-pinion – A form of steering mechanism where the steering wheel moves a pinion gear, which in turn moves a toothed rack connected to the roadwheels.

Radial tyre – A tyre where the fabric material plies (under the tread) are arranged at right-angles to the circumference of the tyre.

Radiator – A cooling device, located in a cooling airflow, through which a hot liquid is passed. A radiator is made up of fine tubes and fins to allow rapid cooling of the liquid inside.

Refrigerant – The substance used to absorb heat in an air conditioning system. The refrigerant is changed from a gas to a liquid and vice versa during the air conditioning process.

Release arm or lever – The device that transmits the movement of the clutch pedal to the clutch release bearing.

Release bearing – A bearing used to operate a clutch. It allows for the fact that the release arm or lever moves laterally, and the clutch components are rotating.

Rev counter – See Tachometer.

Rich – A term used to describe an air/fuel mixture containing more than the optimum amount of fuel.

Rocker arm – A lever used in an engine's valve-operating mechanism which rocks on a central pivot, with one end moved up and down by the camshaft and the other end operating a valve.

Rotor arm – A rotating arm in a distributor, which distributes the HT circuit voltage to the correct spark plug. An electrode on the rotor arm distributes the voltage to electrodes in the distributor cap, which are connected to the HT leads.

Running-on – A tendency for the engine to keep on running after the ignition has been switched off. Often caused by incorrect ignition timing, the wrong grade of fuel, or a poorly maintained engine.

Self-diagnostic system – A system that monitors the operation of an electronically controlled system, and stores a fault code in the system electronic control unit memory if a fault is detected.

Servo – A device for increasing the normal effort applied to a control. A brake servo increases the effort applied by the driver to the brake pedal.

Shim – A thin spacer, often used to adjust the clearance between two parts; for example, shims located under bucket tappets control the valve clearances.

Shock absorber – A device used to damp out the up-and-down movement of a wheel when the car hits a bump in the road.

Single-point fuel injection – A fuel injection system that has a single fuel injector.

16-valve – A term used to describe a four-cylinder engine with four valves per cylinder, usually two exhaust and two inlet valves. Gives improved efficiency due to improved air/fuel mixture and exhaust gas flow in the combustion chambers.

Slave cylinder – A cylinder containing a piston and hydraulic fluid, which receives hydraulic fluid pressure from a master cylinder, via a pipe, and uses movement of the piston to operate a mechanism.

Spark plug – A device that provides the spark in a petrol engine's combustion chamber in order to ignite the air/fuel mixture. The HT circuit voltage jumps between two electrodes on the spark plug, creating a spark.

Spark plug gap – The air gap between the electrodes on a spark plug.

Starter motor – An electric motor used to start the engine. A pinion gear on the starter motor engages with a large gear on the engine's flywheel, which turns the crankshaft.

Steering gear – A general term used to describe the steering components. Usually refers to a steering rack-and-pinion assembly.

Steering rack – See Rack-and-pinion.

Strut – See MacPherson strut.

Stub axle – A short axle that carries one roadwheel.

Subframe – A small frame mounted underneath a car's body that carries the suspension and/or drivetrain assemblies.

Sump – The main reservoir for the engine oil. Bolted to the bottom of the engine.

Supercharger – A device that uses an engine-driven turbine (usually driven from the crankshaft) to drive a compressor which forces air into the engine. This increases the air/fuel mixture flow into the engine and increases the engine's power.

Suppressor – A device used to reduce or eliminate electrical interference caused by the ignition system or other electrical components.

Suspension – A general term used to describe the system that insulates a car's body from the roadwheels, and keeps all four roadwheels in contact with the road surface.

Synchromesh – A device used in a manual gearbox to synchronise the speeds of two gears to produce smooth, quiet engagement of the gears.

Tachometer (rev counter) – Indicates engine speed in revolutions per minute.

Tappet adjustment – See Valve clearance.

Thermostat – A device which aids engine warm-up by preventing the coolant from flowing through the radiator until a pre-determined temperature is reached. The thermostat then regulates the temperature of the coolant.

TPS (Throttle Position Sensor) – A sensor used in an engine management system to provide information on the position of the throttle valve.

Throttle valve – A flap valve on a petrol engine, controlled by the accelerator pedal, located between the air cleaner and the inlet manifold. It controls the amount of air entering the engine.

Tie-rod – See Track-rod.

Timing belt (cam belt) – Toothed drive belt used to transmit drive from the crankshaft to the camshaft(s).

Timing chain – Metal flexible link chain that engages with sprockets, used to transmit drive from the crankshaft to the camshaft(s).

Toe-in/toe-out – The angle at which the front wheels point inwards or outwards from the straight-ahead position when the steering is positioned straight-ahead. Toe-in is when the front edges of the wheels point inwards.

Torque – The turning force generated by a rotating component.

Torque converter – A coupling used in an automatic transmission between the engine's flywheel and the transmission. The driving torque is transmitted through oil inside the torque converter.

Torque wrench – A tool used to tighten fasteners to an exactly measured torque (tightness).

Torsion bar – A metal bar which twists about its own axis. Used in some suspension systems.

Torx – A type of fastener, usually a screw or bolt, which needs a specially-shaped (Torx) socket or key to remove and refit it. Torx fasteners come in various standard sizes.

Track-rod (tie-rod) – A metal rod that connects the steering gear to a hub carrier. The track-rods move the front wheels when the steering wheel is turned.

Trailing arm – A form of independent suspension where the roadwheel is attached to a pivoting arm, with the wheel mounted to the rear of the pivot.

Transaxle – A combined gearbox/differential assembly from which two drive shafts transmit the drive to the wheels.

Transmission – A general term used to describe some or all of the drivetrain components excluding the engine. Commonly used to describe automatic gearboxes.

Turbocharger – A device that uses a turbine driven by the engine exhaust gases to drive a compressor which forces air into the engine.

This increases the air/fuel mixture flow into the engine and increases the engine's power.

Twin-cam – Abbreviation for twin overhead camshafts – see OHC.

Universal joint – A joint that can move in any direction whilst transmitting torque. Used in propeller shafts and some drive shafts. Not suitable for some uses because the input and output shaft speeds are not always the same for all angles of the joint.

Unleaded petrol – Petrol that had no lead added during manufacture, but still has the natural lead content of crude oil.

Vacuum pump – A pump driven by the engine that creates a vacuum to operate the brake servo on a diesel engine.

Valve – A device that opens or closes to stop or allow gas or fluid flow.

Valve clearance – The clearance between the top of a valve and the camshaft, necessary to allow the valve to close fully and to allow for expansion of the valve gear components with temperature. Often adjusted by altering the clearance between the tappet and camshaft.

Valve gear – A general term for the components which are acted on by a camshaft to operate the valves.

Vee-engine – An engine design in which the cylinders are arranged in two rows forming a 'V' when viewed from one end. For example, a V8 has two rows of four cylinders each.

Voltage regulator – A device that regulates the output of the alternator.

Water pump – See Coolant pump.

Wheel alignment – The process of checking the toe-in/toe-out, and sometimes the camber and castor angles of the wheels. On most cars only the toe-in/toe-out can be adjusted. Incorrect wheel alignment can cause tyre wear and poor handling.

Wheel balancing – The process of adding small weights to the rim of a wheel so that there are no out-of-balance forces when the wheel rotates.

Wheel cylinder – A slave cylinder used to operate the brake shoes in a drum brake.

Useful contacts

OFFICIAL BODIES

DVLA
Driver and Vehicle Licensing Agency
Longview Road
Swansea SA6 7JL
Website: www.dvla.gov.uk
Driver enquiries:
Tel: 0300 790 6801
Fax: 0300 123 0784
Vehicle enquiries:
Tel: 0300 790 6802
Fax: 0300 123 0798

DVSA
Driving and Vehicles Standards Agency
The Ellipse
Padley Road
Swansea
SA1 8AN
Tel: 0300 123 9000
Website: www.dsa.gov.uk

MOTORING ORGANISATIONS

AA
AA Customer Support
Fanum House
Basingstoke
Hampshire
RG21 4EA
Tel: 0800 085 2721
Website: www.theaa.com

RAC
RAC Motoring Services
RAC House
1 Forest Road
Brockhurst Crescent
Walsall
WS5 4AW
Tel: 08000 722 822
Website: www.rac.co.uk

Green Flag
Green Flag Rapid Breakdown Cover
The Wharf
Neville Street
Leeds
LS1 4AZ
Tel: 0845 246 1557
Website: www.greenflag.com

IAM
The Institute of Advanced Motorists
IAM House
510 Chiswick High Road
London W4 5RG
Tel: 0845 126 8600
Website: www.iam.org.uk

More manuals from Haynes